HOOKED *for* TODDLERS

HOOKED *for* TODDLERS
20 Easy Crochet Projects

MARGARET HUBERT

Creative Publishing
international

Chanhassen, MN

For my wonderful family, the sunshine of my life

Acknowledgments

I wish to thank Blue Heron Yarns, DMC, Patons Yarns, Plymouth Yarn Company, and Tahki/Stacy Charles, Inc., who so graciously donated yarns for most of the projects in this book.

Thanks to Jeannine Buehler and Paula Alexander for helping me crochet some of the garments. I would also like to thank Linda Neubauer, my editor, who is a joy to work with. Special thanks to my daughter, Sharon Valencia, for allowing me to use her idea in creating the little doll's dress and matching toddler dress.

Creative Publishing international

Copyright 2007
Creative Publishing international
18705 Lake Drive East
Chanhassen, Minnesota 55317
1-800-328-3895
www.creativepub.com
All rights reserved

President/CEO: Ken Fund
Executive Managing Editor: Barbara Harold
Senior Editor: Linda Neubauer
Photo Stylist: Joanne Wawra
Creative Director: Brad Springer
Photo Art Director: Tim Himsel
Photographer: Steve Galvin
Production Manager: Laura Hokkanen
Cover and Book Design: Dania Davey
Page Layout: Lois Stanfield

Due to differing conditions, materials, and skill levels, the publisher and various manufacturers disclaim any liability for unsatisfactory results or injury due to improper use of tools, materials, or information in this publication.

All rights reserved. No part of this work covered by the copyrights hereon may be reproduced or used in any form or by any means—graphic, electronic, or mechanical, including photocopying, recording, taping of information on storage and retrieval systems—without the written permission of the publisher.

Printed in China

10 9 8 7 6 5 4 3 2 1

Library of Congress Cataloging-in-Publication Data

Hubert, Margaret.
 Hooked for toddlers : 20 easy crochet projects / Margaret Hubert.
   p. cm.
 ISBN-13: 978-1-58923-297-6 (soft cover)
 ISBN-10: 1-58923-297-6 (soft cover)
 1. Crocheting--Patterns. 2. Children's clothing. 3. Infants' clothing. I. Title.
 TT825.H7983 2007
 746.43'4041--dc22   2006024649

All the yarns used in this book can be found or ordered at your local yarn shop or craft store. Visit the following web sites for more information about the yarns shown:

Blue Heron Yarns
www.blueheronyarns.com

DMC
www.dmc-usa.com

Dale of Norway
www.dale.no

Patons Yarns
www.patonsyarns.com

Plymouth Yarn Company
www.plymouthyarn.com

Tahki/Stacy Charles, Inc.
www.tahkistacycharles.com

Contents

ABOUT THE PROJECTS	6
Pretty Posies Dress	8
Pretty Posies Hat	14
Two-Piece Dress	16
Halter Top and Shell Skirt	22
Juliet Pouch	26
Grow-a-Year Jumper	28
Little Waves Jumper	32
Cool Stripes Sundress	36
Cool Stripes Doll Dress	42
Easy, Breezy Sleeveless Dress	46
Easy, Breezy Cropped Jacket	50
Color Block Pullover	54
Summer Fun Vest	58
Cool Weather Cardigan	62
Flower Border Cardigan	66
Blue Cables Pullover	72
Blue Cables Beanie	76
Petite Shells Apricot Pullover	78
Cable Loop Hat	82
Multicolor Hoodie	84
CROCHET STITCHES	88
ABBREVIATIONS	96

About the Projects

TODDLER FASHIONS HAVE LONG been a crochet favorite. The versatility of crochet lends itself to a variety of looks. Lacy party dresses, lightweight cardigans, warm jackets, and cute hats can all be achieved with the right choice of yarns, hooks, and a combination of stitches.

I have always thought of myself as a designer of women's fashions, not a designer of children's wear. Over the years, as a mother and grandmother, I have had fun making some unique fashions for the youngsters in my own family. Some of them were published, but it was not the norm. When my granddaughter was three, I made her a very simple little pullover, which she loved but outgrew very quickly. The chest still fit, but the sleeves and body were too short. I found that I could easily add to the body and sleeves by crocheting several rows of a shell pattern. Not only did it give her at least one more year of wear, but it looked great. She is still wearing and loving the sweater at age five.

This experience started the wheels turning, and the grow-a-year concept started taking shape. I wanted to come up with some other ways to add a little more wear time to my handmade children's garments. When I started playing around with this concept, several other ideas came to mind: straps with adjustable buttons, drawstring waists, cuffs. Before I knew it, I had an array of toddler designs in front of me. *Hooked for Toddlers* was born! Not all the styles in the book fit in the grow-a-year category, but any garment can be given new life by adding a few rows to the bottom and sleeves, with either matching or contrasting yarn.

I have included styles for girls and boys; some garments are suitable for both. Often, changing the yarn colors and buttonhole placement is all that is needed. For each item, I chose a yarn to complement the stitch and style. For the little girls' dresses, I chose lightweight cotton yarns because they are strong and durable, easy to care for, and look great in whatever stitch is used. Light and airy shell stitches or single crochet all work well in cotton yarn. For medium weight garments, I chose sport weight yarns. For the heavier weight garments, I chose worsted weight yarns, including easy-care acrylic, wool, and wool blends. The materials list for each project will tell you the weight and type of each yarn, as well as the brands and colors that I used. You can substitute other yarns to create a different look, but you must be sure to get the same gauge when substituting, or your garment will not turn out to be the right size.

Beginners and experienced crocheters alike will have fun with these styles. Most of the patterns use very basic stitches, and I've sprinkled in a few challenging-but-fun stitch patterns for you to enjoy. If you need to learn or review a stitch, just go to "Crochet Stitches" (page 88) for detailed, photographed instructions.

I have had such fun writing this book! Watching the designs take shape—from those first quick sketches to actuality—was a joy. I hope you have as much fun as I did. May your crocheted creations bring smiles to the special toddlers in your life.

MARGARET HUBERT is also the author of *Hooked Bags, Hooked Hats, Hooked Throws, Hooked Scarves, How to Free-Form Crochet,* and six other books. She designs crochet projects for yarn companies and magazines and teaches at yarn shops, retreats, and national gatherings.

Pretty Posies Dress

Little girls love to dress up in something pretty. This delightful little dress has short, ruffled sleeves and a garden of posies on the bodice. Make one for a special little girl in her favorite colors.

PRETTY POSIES DRESS

YARN

Superfine cotton/acrylic yarn

Shown: Senso Microfiber Cotton by DMC, 60% cotton, 40% acrylic, 1.52 oz (43 g)/150 yd (137 m): #1106 (MC), 7 (7, 8) balls; #1108 (CC), 1 ball

HOOKS

4/E (3.5 mm)

5/F (3.75 mm)

STITCHES USED

Single crochet

Double crochet

Reverse single crochet

GAUGE

20 sc = 4" (10 cm) on 5/F hook

NOTIONS

Tapestry needle

Four buttons, ½" (1.3 cm) diameter

Hand-sewing needle

Thread

FINISHED SIZE

18 months (24 months, 2T)

Chest size: 20" (21", 22") [51 (53.5, 56) cm]

Button bands are worked vertically in single crochet at the inner edges of the yoke backs.

Fasten off yarns and restart where noted. Yoke is worked in 3 pieces, each beg at waist and worked to shoulder. Skirt is then picked up at waist and worked downward in rnds. See page 93 for making chain loop flowers.

FRONT YOKE

Foundation row: Using 5/F hook and MC, ch 49 (51, 53). Pull up lp with CC; fasten off MC.

Row 1 (WS, leaf row): With CC, ch 1 (counts as sc), sk first ch, work 1 sc in each of next 8 (9, 10) ch, * [in next ch (sc, ch 8, sc) 3 times], 1 sc in each of next 9 ch, rep from * 2 times more, then rep bet [ ] once, end 1 sc in each of last 9 (10, 11) ch (4 lp CL). Pull up lp with MC, fasten off CC, turn.

Row 2: With MC, ch 1 (counts as sc), sk first sc, work 1 sc in each of next 8 (9, 10) sc, * ch 1, sk lps, 1 sc in each of next 9 sc, rep from * 3 times more, end 1 sc in each of last 8 (9, 10) sc, turn—49 (51, 53) sc.

Row 3: Ch 1 (counts as sc), sk first sc, work 1 sc in each of next 5 (6, 7) sc, * 1 sc in next sc and through right ch lp, catching it in place, 1 sc in each of next 2 sc, 1 sc in ch-1 sp, 1 sc in each of next 2 sc, 1 sc in next sc and through left ch lp, catching it in place, 1 sc in each of next 3 sc, rep from * 3 times more, end 1 sc in each of last 2 (3, 4) sc, 1 sc in tch, turn.

Row 4: Ch 1 (counts as sc), sk first sc, work 1 sc in each sc across, turn— 49 (51, 53) sc.

Row 5 (WS, flower row): Ch 1 (counts as sc), sk first sc, work 1 sc in each of next 8 (9, 10) sc, * 6 dc in next sc and through center lp, catching it in place, 1 sc in each of next 9 sc, rep from * 3 times more, end 1 sc in each of last 8 (9, 10) sc, 1 sc in top of tch, turn—4 flower CL.

Row 6: Ch 1 (counts as sc), sk first sc, work 1 sc in each of next 8 (9, 10) sc, * ch 1, sk the dcs, 1 sc in each of next 9 sc, rep from * 3 times more, end 1 sc in each of last 8 (9, 10) sc, 1 sc in top of tch—49 (51, 53) sc. Pull up lp with CC, fasten off MC, turn.

Row 7: With CC, ch 1 (counts as sc), sk first sc, work 1 sc in each of next 3 (4, 5) sc, * [in next sc (sc, ch 8, sc) 3 times], 1 sc in each of next 4 sc, 1 sc in ch-1 sp, 1 sc in each of next 4 sc, rep from * 4 times more, end 1 sc in each of last 3 (4, 5) sc, 1 sc in tch. Pull up lp with MC, fasten off CC, turn.

Row 8: With MC, ch 1 (counts as sc), sk first sc, work 1 sc in each of next 3 (4, 5) sc, * ch 1, sk lps, 1 sc in each of next 9 sc, rep from * 3 times more, ch 1, sk lps, 1 sc in each of last 4 (5, 6) sc, turn.

Row 9: Ch 1 (do not sk a sc, do not count this ch-1 as first sc), work 1 sc in each of next 1 (2, 3) sc, * 1 sc in next sc and through lp, catching it in place, 1 sc in each of next 2 sc, 1 sc in ch-1 sp, 1 sc in each of next 2 sc, 1 sc in next sc and lp, catching it in place, 1 sc in each of next 3 sc, rep from * 4 times more, end 1 sc in each of last 1 (2, 3) sc, turn.

Row 10: Ch 1 (counts as sc), sk first sc, work 1 sc in each sc across row, 1 sc in tch, turn—49 (51, 53) sc.

Row 11: Ch 1 (counts as sc), sk first sc, work 1 sc in each of next 3 (4, 5) sc, * 6 dc in next sc and through lp, catching it in place, 1 sc in each of next 9 sc, rep from * 4 times more, end 1 sc in each of last 3 (4, 5) sc, 1 sc in tch, turn.

Row 12: Ch 1 (counts as sc), sk first sc, work 1 sc in each of next 3 (4, 5) sc, * ch 1, sk dcs, 1 sc in each of next 9 sc, rep from * 4 times more, end ch 1, sk dcs, 1 sc in each of last 4 (5, 6) sc. Pull up lp with CC; fasten off MC.

Rep rows 1–12 one time more, then rep rows 1 to 6.

SHAPE NECK
Left front
Row 1: Using 5/F hook and MC, ch 1 (counts as sc), sk first sc, work 1 sc in each of next 16 (17, 18) sts, turn.

Row 2: Ch 1 (counts as sc), sc2tog, work 1 sc in each of next 14 (15, 16) sts—16 (17, 18) sts rem—turn.

Row 3: Ch 1 (counts as sc), sk first sc, work 1 sc in each of rem 15 (16, 17) sc, turn.

Rows 4, 5, and 6: Rep row 3 (fasten off for size 18 months).

Rows 7 and 8: Rep row 3 (fasten off for size 24 months).

Rows 9 and 10: Rep row 3 (fasten off for size 2T).

Right front
Sk center 15 sts, join MC, work rem 17 (18, 19) sc on right side to correspond to left side, reversing shaping.

BACK YOKE
Right back
Foundation row: Using 5/F hook and MC, ch 26 (27, 28).

Row 1: Starting in second ch from hook, work 1 sc in each ch to end, turn—25 (26, 27) sc.

Row 2: Ch 1 (counts as sc), sk first sc, work 1 sc in each sc to end, turn.

Rep row 2 until front is 1" (2.5 cm) shorter than front to shoulder, Sl st over 10 sc, work rem 15 (16, 17) sc, ch 1, turn.

Next row: Sc2tog, cont working in sc until back is same length as front to shoulder.

Left back
Same as right back, reversing shaping. Sew front to backs at shoulders.

SKIRT
Using 5/F hook and MC, with RS facing, starting at back edge, sc 25 (26, 27) sts at bottom of yoke, ch 5, sc 48 (50, 52) sts along bottom of front yoke, ch 5, sc 25 (26, 27) sts along bottom of rem back yoke, turn—108 (112, 116) sts.

Next row: Ch 3, work 1 row dc, inc every other st, turn—162 (168, 174) sts. Join with Sl st to other side and from here on, work in rnds.

Rnd 1: Ch 1, 1 sc in each dc around, join with Sl st to beg ch 1.

Rnd 2: Ch 3, 1 dc in each sc around, join with Sl st to third ch of beg ch 3.

Rep rnds 1 and 2 until skirt is 12" (12½", 13") [30.5 (31.8, 33) cm] from waistline; fasten off.

SLEEVES
Make 2.

Foundation row: Using 5/F hook and MC, ch 71 (73, 75).

Row 1 (WS): Starting in second ch from hook, work 1 sc in each ch across, turn—70 (72, 74) sc.

Row 2: Ch 3 (counts as dc), sk first st, work 1 dc in each st across, turn.

Row 3 (dec row): Ch 1 (counts as sc), sk first st, sc2tog across, work 1 sc in tch, turn—36 (37, 38) sc.

Row 4: Ch 3 (counts as dc), work 1 dc in each st across, turn.

Row 5: Sl st over 2 sts, ch 1, work 1 sc in each of next 32 (33, 34) sts, leaving last 2 sts not worked, turn.

Row 6: Ch 3 (counts as dc), sk first sc, work 1 dc in each sc across, 1 dc in tch, turn.

Row 7: Ch 1 (counts as sc), sk first dc, work 1 sc in each dc across, 1 sc in tch, turn.

Rows 8, 10, and 12: Rep row 6.

Rows 9 and 11: Rep row 7.

Row 13: Ch 1 (counts as sc), sc2tog, sc to last 3 sts, sc2tog, work 1 sc in top of tch, turn.

Row 14: Ch 3 (counts as dc), dc2tog, dc to last 3 sts, dc2tog, work 1 dc in top of tch, turn.

Rows 15, 17, and 19: Rep row 13.

Rows 16 and 18: Rep row 14—18 (19, 20) sts rem after row 18.

Next row: Sc2tog across row; fasten off.

BUTTON BANDS
Right back
Row 1: Using 4/E hook and MC, starting at neck edge, with RS facing you, work 30 (31, 32) sc along side of back opening, turn.

Row 2: Ch 1, sk first sc, work 1 sc in each st to end, turn.

Row 3: Rep row 2; fasten off.

Left back
Row 1: Using 4/E hook and MC, starting at bottom of opening, with RS facing you, work 30 (31, 32) sc to top, turn.

Row 2 (buttonhole row): Ch 1, sk first sc, work 1 sc in next sc, ch 2, sk 2 sc, * 1 sc in each of next 6 sc, ch 2, sk 2 sc, rep from * 2 times more, sc to end of row, turn.

Row 3: Ch 1, sk first sc, work 1 sc in each st and 2 sc in each ch-2 sp to end; do not fasten off.

Work 3 sc in corner to turn, cont in sc around neck edge to other side, do not turn. Work 1 row rev sc around neck edge only; fasten off.

FINISHING
1. Weave in ends, using tapestry needle.
2. Overlap button bands. Sew them together at bottom, using tapestry needle and single strand of yarn.
3. Sew underarm sleeve seams.
4. Pin sleeves to dress, matching center top of sleeve to shoulder seam and bottom seam to underarm. Sew in sleeves.
5. Sew on buttons, using a hand-sewing needle and thread.

Pretty Posies Hat

Crochet a darling little hat to keep the sun out of her eyes. Made of cool cotton, this little noggin topper is comfortable and lightweight, perfect for a summer stroll.

CROWN

With MC, ch 69 (71, 73). Work posy patt as for yoke of dress (page 10) until 6 rows are completed, turn.

Row 7: Ch 3, work 1 dc in each st, do not turn, join work at top of beg ch 3, cont working in rnds as for skirt (page 12). Work 1 row sc, 1 row dc, until 3" (3½", 4") [7.5 (9, 10) cm] from beg, ending with sc row.

First dec rnd: Dec 0 (2, 4) sts evenly spaced across row—70 sts all sizes.

Second dec rnd: * Work 1 sc in each of next 8 dc, sc2tog, rep from * 6 times more—62 sc.

Third dec rnd: * Work 1 dc in each of next 7 sc, dc2tog, rep from * 6 times more—55 dc.

Fourth dec rnd: * Work 1 sc in each of next 6 dc, sc2tog, rep from * 6 times more—48 sc.

Fifth dec rnd: * Work 1 dc in each of next 5 sc, dc2tog, rep from * 6 times more—41 dc.

Sixth dec rnd: * Work 1 sc in each of next 4 dc, sc2tog, rep from * 6 times more—34 sc.

Seventh dec rnd: * Work 1 dc in each of next 3 sc, dc2tog, rep from * 6 times more—27 dc.

Eighth dec rnd: * Sc2tog, rep from * to end; fasten off, leaving yarn tail for sewing. Thread tapestry needle with yarn tail and gather top of hat tog.

BRIM

Sew back seam where posy patt was worked before rnds started.

With RS facing you, join MC at bottom back, ch 1, work 2 sc in each st around, join with Sl st to beg ch 1, do not turn—138 (140, 142) sc.

Work 4 rnds as foll: 1 rnd dc, 1 rnd sc, 1 rnd dc, 1 rnd sc, fasten off.

PRETTY POSIES HAT

YARN

Superfine cotton/acrylic yarn

Shown: Senso Microfiber Cotton by DMC, 60% cotton, 40% acrylic, 1.52 oz (43 g)/150 yd (137 m): #1106 (MC), 1 ball; #1108 (CC), 1 ball

HOOK

5/F (3.75 mm)

STITCHES USED

Single crochet

Double crochet

GAUGE

20 sc = 4" (10 cm)

NOTION

Tapestry needle

FINISHED SIZE

14" (14½", 15") [35.6 (36.8, 38.1) cm] head circumference

Fits tightest above the ears; spreads wider into brim.

Two-Piece Dress

This dainty two-piece dress is also very practical. A delicate shell stitch pattern is used for the skirt and sleeves. The top and skirt button together at the waist, so the length can be adjusted as the little girl grows.

TWO-PIECE DRESS

YARN

Lightweight cotton yarn

Shown: Grace by Patons, 100% cotton, 1.75 oz (50 g)/136 yd (125 m): Sweetpea #60230, 4 (5, 5) skeins

HOOKS

5/F (3.75 mm)//
6/G (4 mm)//
7 (4.5 mm) (for size 2T only)

STITCHES USED

Single crochet//
Double crochet//
Shell stitch//
V stitch

GAUGE

2½ shells and 2 V patterns = 4" (10 cm) using 5/F hook

2 shells and 2 V patterns = 4" (10 cm) using 6/G hook

17 sc = 4" (10 cm) using 6/G hook

NOTIONS

Tapestry needle

One button for back of neck, ⅜" (1 cm) diameter

12 buttons for waistline, ¾" (2 cm) diameter

Hand-sewing needle

Thread

FINISHED SIZE

18 months (24 months, 2T)

Chest size: 20" (21", 22") [51 (53.5, 56) cm]

STITCH PATTERNS
Shell stitch: 3 dc, ch 1, 3 dc all in same st or sp
V stitch: 1 dc, ch 1, 1 dc all in same st or sp

Skirt starts at waist and is worked in rnds to hem. Bodice starts at waist and is worked in parts: front, back, and sleeves.

SKIRT
Skirt patt is same for all sizes. Change sizes by changing hook size for shell patt rnds.

With 5/F hook, ch 100. Join with Sl st, being careful not to twist, pm for back seam.

Foundation rnd: Ch 1, work 1 sc in each ch, join with Sl st to beg ch 1.

Rnd 1: Ch 3, work 1 dc in each st, join with Sl st to top of beg ch 3.

Rnd 2: Ch 1, work 1 sc in each st.

Rnds 3 and 5: Rep rnd 1.

Rnd 4: Rep rnd 2.

Rnd 6: Rep rnd 2, inc every fifth st to 120 sts.

Change to 6/G (6/G, 7) hook and beg shell patt as foll:

Rnd 1: Ch 3 (counts as half of V st), sk 2 sc, * make shell of [3 dc, ch 1, 3 dc] in next st, sk 2, make V st of [1 dc, ch 1, 1 dc] in next st, rep from * 18 times more, end 1 shell, sk 2, 1 dc in same st as beg ch 3, ch 1, join with Sl st to top of beg ch 3 (this completes V st)—20 shells in all.

Rnd 2: Ch 3 (counts as dc), work 2 dc in same st as ch 3 (counts as half shell), * 1 V st in next ch-1 sp of shell, 1 shell in ch-1 sp of V st, rep from * 18 times more, end 1 V st in ch-1 sp of last shell, 3 dc in same sp as beg ch (this completes shell), ch 1, join with Sl st to top of beg ch 3.

Rep rnds 1 and 2 until skirt is 10½" (11", 11½") [26.7 (28, 29.3) cm] from beg; fasten off.

BODICE FRONT
Foundation row: With 6/G hook, ch 48 (50, 52). Starting in second ch from hook, work 1 sc in each ch across, turn—48 (50, 52) sts.

Row 1 (RS): Ch 1 (counts as sc), sk first st, work 1 sc in each st across, 1 sc in tch, turn—47 (49, 51) sts.

Row 2: Ch 4 (counts as 1 dc, ch 1), sk 2 sts, work 1 dc next st, * ch 1, sk 1, 1 dc in next st, rep from * across, turn—23 (24, 25) ch-1 sps.

Alternating shell stitches and V stitches create the delicate, lacy fabric of the skirt and sleeves. Rows of double crochet stitches separated by chain-1 spaces make up the adjustable "buttonholes" at the bottom of the bodice.

Row 3: Ch 1, work 1 sc in each dc and in each ch-1 sp across, end 1 sc in last sp, 1 sc in top of tch, turn—47 (49, 51) sts.

Rows 4 and 6: Rep row 2.

Rows 5 and 7: Rep row 3.

Cont to rep row 3 until piece is 3" (3½", 4") [7.5 (9, 10) cm] from beg.

Shape armholes as foll: Sl st over 4 sts, sc in each st across to within 4 sts of end—39 (41, 43) sc—ch 1, turn.

First dec row: Ch 1, sk first st, sc2tog (dec made), sc in each st across to within 3 sts of end, sc2tog, sc in top of tch, turn—37 (39, 41) sts.

Second dec row: Ch 1, rep last row one time more, turn—35 (37, 39) sts.

Work even in sc on 35 (37, 39) sts until armhole is 2½" (3", 3½") [6.5 (7.5, 9) cm].

Shape left neck edge: ch 1 (counts as sc), sk first st, work 1 sc in each of next 10 (11, 12) sts, turn—11 (12, 13) sts.

Ch 1 (counts as sc), sk first st, sc2tog, work 1 sc in each st across, turn—10 (11, 12) sts.

Ch 1 (counts as sc), sk first st, work 1 sc in each of next 7 (8, 9) sts, sc2tog, 1 sc in top of tch—9 (10, 11) sts.

Work even in sc on rem 9 (10, 11) sts, until armhole is 4½" (5", 5½") [11.5 (12.7, 14) cm]; fasten off.

Shape right neck edge: sk center 13 (13, 13) sts, join yarn, and work rem 12 sts to correspond to left neck edge, reversing all shaping.

BODICE BACK

Work same as bodice front until armhole is 3" (3½", 4") [7.5 (9, 10) cm] from beg. At this point, back is divided in half to leave a small opening for pulling over head.

Left back (WS): Sc across 17 (18, 19) sts, turn. Cont to work sc on these 17 (18, 19) sts until armhole is 4" (4½", 5") [10 (11.5, 12.7) cm], ending at neck edge. Sl st over 6 sts, work 1 sc in each of rem 11 (12, 13) sts. Work 2 more rows on rem sts, dec at neck edge each row; fasten off.

Right back (WS): Sk 1 st at center, join yarn, work rem 17 (18, 19) sts to correspond to left back, reversing all shaping.

SLEEVES

Make 2. Sleeve starts at top and is worked down.

Row 1: With 6/G hook, ch 17. Work 1 dc in fifth ch from hook (counts as V st), * sk 2 ch, [2 dc, ch 1, 2 dc] in next ch, sk 2 ch, [1 dc, ch 1, 1 dc] in next ch, rep from * one time more, turn—3 V sts and 2 shells.

Row 2: Ch 3, work [1 dc, ch 1, 1 dc] in next ch-1 sp, * [1 dc, ch 1, 1 dc] in next ch-1 sp (V st), [3 dc, ch 1, 3 dc] in next ch-1 sp (shell), rep from * one time more, [1 dc, ch 1, 1 dc] in next ch-1 sp, [1 dc, ch 1, 1 dc] in next ch-1 sp, 1 dc in top of tch, turn.

Row 3: Ch 3, work 1 V st in ch-1 sp of first V st, * 1 shell in ch-1 sp of next V st, 1 V st in ch-1 sp of next shell, rep from * one time more, 1 shell in ch-1 sp of next V st, 1 V st in ch-1 sp of last V st, 1 dc in top of tch, turn.

Row 4: Ch 3, * work [2 dc, ch 1, 2 dc] in first V st, * 1 V st in ch-1 sp of next shell, 1 shell in ch-1 sp of next V st, rep from * one time more, 1 V st in ch-1 sp of next shell, [2 dc, ch 1, 2 dc] in ch-1 sp of last V st, end 1 dc in top of tch, turn.

Row 5: Ch 3, * work 1 V st in ch-1 sp of next shell, 1 shell in ch-1 sp of next V st, rep from * 2 times more, end 1 V st, 1 dc in top of tch, turn.

Row 6: Ch 3, * work 1 shell in ch-1 sp of next V st, 1 V st in ch-1 sp of next shell, rep from * 2 times more, end 1 shell, 1 dc in top of tch, turn.

Row 7: Ch 3, work 1 dc in same st as ch 3, * 1 V st in ch-1 sp of next shell, 1 shell in ch-1 sp of next V st, rep from * 2 times more, end 1 V st in ch-1 sp of next shell, [1 dc, ch 1, 1 dc] in top of tch, turn.

Row 8: Change to 7 hook for 2T size only. Ch 3, work 1 V st in ch-1 sp, * 1 shell in ch-1 sp of next V st, 1 V st in ch-1 sp of next shell, rep from * 2 times more, end 1 shell, 1 V st in ch-1 sp, 1 dc in top of tch, turn.

Row 9: Ch 3, work 1 V st in ch-1 sp of first V st, * 1 V st in ch-1 sp of shell, 1 shell in ch-1 sp of V st, rep from * 2 times more, end 1 V st in ch-1 sp of shell, 1 V st in ch-1 sp of last V st, 1 dc in top of tch, turn.

Row 10: Ch 3, work 1 V st in ch-1 sp of first V st, * 1 shell in ch-1 sp of next V st, 1 V st in ch-1 sp of next shell, rep from * 3 times more, end 1 dc in top of tch, turn.

Row 11: Ch 3, work 1 dc in same st as ch 3 , * 1 shell in ch-1 sp of V st, 1 V st in ch-1 sp of shell, rep from * 3 times more, end 1 shell in ch-1 sp of V st, 2 dc in top of tch, turn.

Row 12: Ch 3, work 2 dc in same st as ch 3, * 1 V st in ch-1 sp of shell, 1 shell in ch-1 sp of V st, rep from * across, end 1 V st in ch-1 sp of last shell, 3 dc in top of tch; fasten off.

FINISHING
1. Weave in ends, using tapestry needle.
2. Sew shoulder and side seams of bodice. Sew bottom of sleeves for 1" (2.5 cm).
3. Pin center top of sleeve to shoulder seam, pin underarm seams in place, then sew sleeve to bodice.
4. Work neck trim as follows: Starting at top left back opening, RS facing you, work in sc down one side of opening, up other side to neck, 3 sc in corner st, cont around neck back to where you started, turn. Ch 7, Sl st in first st (this forms button lp), work 1 sc in each st around neck, but not down opening, turn. Work 1 sc in first st, * ch 3, 1 sc in each of next 2 sts, rep from * around neck opening; fasten off.
5. Sew small button at top of left back.
6. Sew 12 buttons evenly spaced in center of skirt waistband.

Halter Top and Shell Skirt

Here's a terrific outfit for hot summer days. The ruffly halter top and lacy shell skirt are cool and comfortable, made from easy-care cotton yarn. Quick and easy halter tops go great with shorts too.

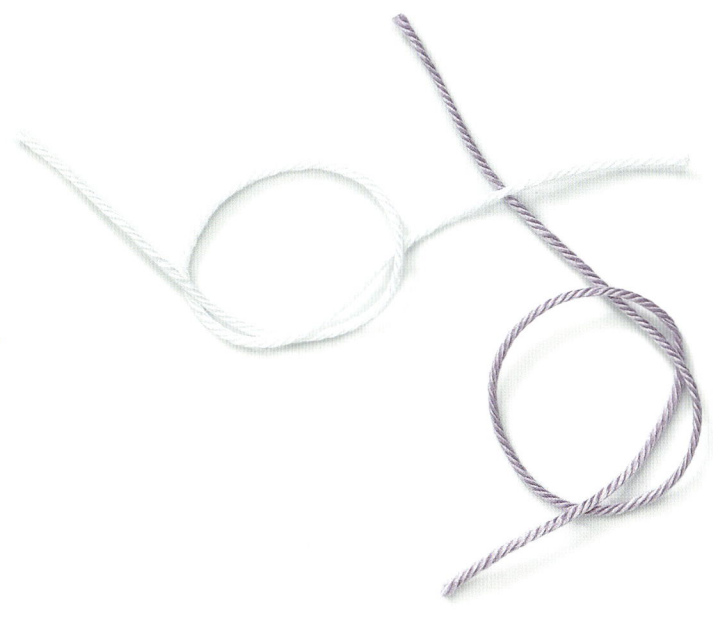

HALTER TOP AND SHELL SKIRT

YARN

Lightweight cotton yarn

Shown: Grace by Patons, 100% cotton, 1.75 oz (50 g)/136 yd (125 m): Lilac #60321 (A), 4 (4, 5) skeins; Snow #60005 (B), 1 skein

HOOKS

5/F (3.75 mm)
6/G (4 mm)
7 (4.5 mm)

STITCHES USED

Single crochet

Single crochet through the back loop

Double crochet

Front post double crochet

Shell stitch

GAUGE

20 sc = 4" (10 cm) using 6/G hook

2 FPdc, (3 dc, ch 1, 3 dc), 2 FPdc, (3 dc, ch 1, 3 dc) = 4" (10 cm) using 6/G hook

NOTION

Tapestry needle

FINISHED SIZE

18 months (24 months, 2T)

Chest size: 19" (20", 21") [48.5 (51, 53.5) cm]

Waist size: 20" (21", 22") [51 (53.5, 56) cm]

Ties make sizes adjustable.

Front post double crochet stitches form ridges between shells on the skirt.

SKIRT

Patt is same for all sizes. Change sizes by changing hook size as directed.

Foundation rnd: Starting at waistband with 5/F (5/F, 6/G) hook and A, ch 122 (128, 128). Being careful not to twist, join with Sl st to form ring.

Rnd 1: Ch 5 (counts as dc, ch 2), * sk 2 ch, work 1 dc in next ch, ch 2, rep from * around, join with Sl st to third ch of beg ch 5—41 (43, 43) ch-2 sps.

Rnd 2: Ch 1, work 2 sc in first ch-2 sp, * 1 sc in next dc, 2 sc in next ch-2 sp, rep from * around, join with Sl st to beg ch 1.

Rnd 3: Ch 3 (counts as dc), sk 2 sc, * work [3 dc, ch 1, 3 dc] in next sc (shell made), sk 2 sc, 1 dc in next sc, ch 1, sk 1 sc, 1 dc in next sc, rep from * 14 (15, 15) times more, end 1 dc, ch 1, join with Sl st to top of beg ch 3—15 (16, 16) shells.

Rnd 4: Ch 3 (counts as dc), work [3 dc, ch 1, 3 dc] in ch-1 sp of next shell, 1 FPdc around post of next dc, ch 1, 1 FPdc around post of next dc, rep from * 14 (15, 15) times more, end 1 FPdc around post of last dc, ch 1, join with Sl st to top of beg ch 3.

Rnds 5 and 6: Rep rnd 4.

Rnds 7–15: Change to 6/G (6/G, 7) hook and rep rnd 4.

Rnd 16: Ch 3 (counts as dc), work [4 dc, ch 1, 4 dc] in ch-1 sp of next shell, 1 FPdc around post of next dc, ch 1, 1 FPdc around post of next dc, rep from * 14 (15, 15) times more, end 1 FPdc around post of last dc, ch 1, join with Sl st to top of beg ch 3.

Rep rnd 16 until 10" (10½", 11") [25.5 (26.7, 28) cm] from beg; fasten off.

WAIST TIE

With 5/F hook and double strand of A, ch 150 (150, 160); fasten off. Starting at center front, weave in and out of open row at waistband.

HALTER TOP

Foundation row: With 6/G hook and B, beg at top, ch 25 (25, 27).

Row 1: Starting in second ch from hook, work 1 sc in each ch across, turn—24 (24, 26) sts.

Row 2: Ch 1 (counts as sc), sk first st, work 2 sc in next st (inc made), 1 sc in each of next 22 (22, 24) sts, 2 sc in next st (inc made), sc in top of tch, turn—26 (26, 28) sts.

Chain-stitch ruffles are attached to ridges on the halter that are formed by working through the back loop.

Row 3: Ch 1 (counts as sc), sk first st, work 1 sc in each st across, 1 sc in top of tch, turn.

Row 4: Rep row 2.

Row 5: Rep row 3.

Row 6: Ch 1 (counts as sc), sk first st, 2 sc tbl in next st (inc made), 1 sc tbl in each st until next to last st, 2 sc tbl in this st, 1 sc in top of tch, turn.

Rep rows 1–6, continuing to inc 1 st each side every other row, and working sixth row each time tbl (this forms ridge on which you will make ruffles), until there are 54 (56, 58) sts. Work rows 1–4 again; fasten off.

TIES

With 5/F hook and B, ch 60 (60, 70) for waist tie, join at bottom left corner with RS facing you, sc along left side to top, ch 60 (60, 70) for first neck tie, sc in each ch, cont sc along top edge, ch 60 (60, 70) for second neck tie, sc in each ch, cont sc along right side, ch 60 (60, 70) for second waist tie, sc in each ch, cont sc along bottom to end of first waist tie; fasten off.

RUFFLES

With 5/F hook and A, join in first st of top ridge. * Ch 3, 1 sc tfl of next st, rep from * across, join with Sl st to last st; fasten off. Rep on each ridge.

Juliet Pouch

Any little girl would love to carry her treasures in this ruffled drawstring pouch. It can be made to match any outfit. One skein of yarn and a small amount of a contrasting color for the ruffles are all it takes.

POUCH

Starting at bottom of bag, ch 3, join with Sl st to form ring.

Foundation rnd: Work 8 sc in ring, pm for beg of rnds, bring up marker at end of each rnd, do not join after each rnd.

Rnd 1: Sc around, inc in every st—16 sc.

Rnd 2: Inc every other st—24 sc.

Rnd 3: Inc every third st—32 sc.

Rnd 4: Inc every fourth st—40 sc.

Cont to inc 8 sts every rnd in this manner, always having 1 more st bet inc, until you have 64 sts.

Rnd 1 of bag body: Work 1 sc tbl of each st around (this forms ridge on which you will make ruffles).

Rnd 2-6: Work 1 sc in each st around.

Rep rnds 1–6 four times more.

Next rnd: Ch 4 (counts as dc, ch 1), * sk 1 st, work 1 dc in next st, ch 1, rep from * around, end ch 1, join with Sl st to third ch of beg ch 4—32 ch-1 sps.

Next rnd: Work 2 sc in each ch-1 sp—64 sc.

Beg shell st patt as foll: ch 3 to start rnd (counts as dc), sk 2 sts, * work [2 dc, ch 2, 2 dc] in next st (shell made), sk 2, 1 dc in each of next 2 sts, rep from * 9 times more, end sk 2, 1 dc in next st, join with Sl st to top of beg ch 3—10 shells.

Next rnd: Ch 3, * work [2 dc, ch 2, 2 dc] in ch-2 sp of next shell, 1 FPdc over each of next 2 dc, rep from * 9 times more, end with FPdc over last dc, join with Sl st to top of beg ch 3; fasten off.

RUFFLES

With CC, join in first st of top ridge and work as foll: * ch 3, work 1 sc tfl of next st, rep from * around, join with Sl st to first st; fasten off. Rep on each ridge.

DRAWSTRINGS

Make 2.
Using double strand of MC, ch 110; fasten off.

Weave drawstrings through openwork rnd at base of shell patt. Tie ends tog to form lp. Rep with rem tie in opposite direction.

JULIET POUCH

YARN

Lightweight cotton yarn

Shown: Grace by Patons, 100% cotton, 1.75 oz (50 g)/136 yd (125 m): Snow #60005 (MC), 1 skein; Lilac #60321 (CC), 1 skein

HOOK

5/F (3.75 mm)

STITCHES USED

Single crochet

Single crochet through the back loop

Double crochet

Front post double crochet

Shell stitch

GAUGE

20 sc = 4" (10 cm)

NOTION

Tapestry needle

FINISHED SIZE

Approximately 6" × 6" (15 × 15 cm)

Grow-a-Year Jumper

Made in comfy cotton yarn, this little jumper can be paired with a T-shirt or worn as a sundress. Multiple buttons on the shoulder straps make it easy to adjust the length. The jumper is crocheted from the top down, so you can always add a few more rows at the bottom after a growth spurt.

GROW-A-YEAR JUMPER

YARN
Medium-weight cotton yarn

Shown: Cotton Classic II by Tahki/Stacy Charles, 100% cotton, 1.75 oz (50 g)/74 yd (68 m): turquoise #2815 (A), 3 skeins; periwinkle #2882 (B), 1 skein; green #2726 (C), 1 skein

HOOK
8/H (5 mm)

STITCHES USED
Single crochet

Double crochet

GAUGE
15 sc = 4" (10 cm) in bodice pattern

13 sc = 4" (10 cm) in skirt pattern

NOTIONS
Tapestry needle

Six buttons, ½" (1.3 cm) diameter

Hand-sewing needle

Thread

FINISHED SIZE
18 months (24 months, 2T)

Chest size: 21" (22", 24") [53.5 (56, 61) cm]

Simple pattern of chain stitch, skipped stitch, and single crochet, worked in rows of alternating colors, gives the bodice an intricate look.

FRONT BODICE

When changing colors, always pull up lp with new color, ch 1, then beg row. Do not end colors at ends of rows. Using 3 alternating colors, you will pick them up again on foll rows.

Foundation row: With A, ch 40 (44, 48). Work 1 sc in fourth ch from hook (counts as sc, ch-1 sp), * ch 1, sk 1, 1 sc in next ch, rep from * 16 (18, 20) times more, turn—18 (20, 22) ch-1 sps.

Row 1: With B, ch 1, sk first sc, * work 1 sc in ch-1 sp, ch 1, sk next sc, rep from * 17 times more, end 1 sc in top of tch, turn.

Row 2: With C, rep row 1.

Rep row 1, alternating A, B, and C, until bodice is 4" (4½", 5") [10 (11.5, 12.7) cm] from beg, ending with A. Fasten off B and C; cont with A to bottom of skirt.

SKIRT

Row 1: Ch 1 (counts as sc), sk first st, * work 2 sc in next ch-1 sp, 1 sc in next sc, rep from * across, end 1 sc in tch, turn—55 (59, 63) sc.

Row 2: Ch 3 (counts as dc), sk first sc, work 1 dc in each sc across, 1 dc in tch, turn—55 (59, 63) dc.

Row 3: Ch 1 (counts as sc), sk first dc, work 1 sc in each dc across, 1 sc in tch, turn—55 (59, 63) sc.

Rep rows 2 and 3 until skirt is 12" (12½", 13") [30.5 (31.8, 33) cm] from bottom of bodice; fasten off.

JUMPER BACK
Work same as front.

STRAPS
Left front strap: with B, RS facing you, sk 7 (7, 8) sts from underarm, join yarn.

Row 1: Work 1 sc in each of next 4 sts, turn.

Row 2: Ch 1 (counts as sc), sk first st, work 1 sc in each of next 3 sc, turn.

Rep row 2 until strap is 4" (4½", 5") [10 (11.5, 12.7) cm]; fasten off.

Right front strap: sk 16 (17, 18) sts for center front, join yarn, and work right front strap to correspond with left front strap.

To lengthen the straps, simply shift the buttonholes.

Back straps: in corresponding placement, work same as front straps until 4" (4½", 5") [10 (11.5, 12.7) cm] long.

First buttonhole, row 1: Ch 1, work 1 sc in first sc, ch 2, sk 2, 1 sc in last sc, turn.

Row 2: Ch 1, work 1 sc in first sc, 2 sc in ch-2 sp, 1 sc in last sc, turn.

Work 4 rows using sc patt as established.

Rep last 6 rows, 2 times more—3 buttonholes in all.

Work 2 more rows in sc; fasten off.

FINISHING
1. Sew side seams, using tapestry needle. Weave in ends.
2. With color B, starting at right underarm seam, work 1 row sc, to first strap, all around strap, across center back, around other strap, to next strap, around strap, across center front, around other strap, back to where you started, join with Sl st; fasten off.
3. With B, join yarn at a seam at bottom of skirt. Work 1 row sc in each st around; fasten off.
4. Sew buttons on front straps to correspond to buttonholes.

Little Waves Jumper

This loose-fitting jumper can be worn alone or over a T-shirt. The tie at the waist and the adjustable straps allow room for growth. Because it is made from the top down, adjusting length is easy, too, so the jumper should fit for at least two years.

LITTLE WAVES JUMPER

YARN
Superfine cotton/acrylic yarn

Shown: Senso Microfiber Cotton by DMC, 60% cotton, 40% acrylic, 1.52 oz (43 g)/150 yd (137 m): #1109 (MC), 4 (4, 5) balls; #1101 (CC), 1 ball

HOOKS
4/E (3.5 mm) for 18 and 24 month sizes

5/F (3.75 mm) for 2T size

STITCHES USED
Single crochet

Double crochet

Half double crochet

Triple crochet

GAUGE
22 dc = 4" (10 cm) using 4/E hook

20 dc = 4" (10 cm) using 5/F hook

NOTIONS
Tapestry needle

Six buttons, ½" (1.3 cm) diameter

Hand-sewing needle

Thread

FINISHED SIZE
18 months (24 months, 2T)

Chest size: 19" (20", 21") [48.5 (51, 53.5) cm]

Waves form as stitches go from single to half double, to double, to triple crochet, and back again.

YOKE

Make 2. Do not end colors at ends of rows. Carry yarn loosely up sides.

Row 1: With 4/E (4/E, 5/F) hook and MC, ch 61. Starting in second ch from hook, work 1 sc in each ch across, turn—60 sc.

Row 2: Ch 1 (counts as sc), sk first sc, work 1 sc in each sc across, turn, do not fasten off MC—60 sc.

Row 3: Ch 3 with CC (counts as dc), sk first sc, work 1 dc in each of next 2 sc, 1 hdc in next sc, 1 sc in next sc, * ch 2, sk 2 sc, 1 sc in next sc, 1 hdc in next sc, 1 dc in each of next 2 sc, 1 tr in each of next 2 sc, 1 dc in each of next 2 sc, 1 hdc in next sc, 1 sc in next sc, rep from * 3 times more to last 7 sc, ch 2, sk 2, 1 sc in next sc, 1 hdc in next sc, 1 dc in each of last 2 sc, 1 tr in top of tch, turn.

Row 4: Ch 3, sk first dc, work 1 dc in each of next 2 dc, 1 hdc in next hdc, 1 sc in next sc, * ch 2, 1 sc in next sc, 1 hdc in next hdc, 1 dc in each of next 2 dc, 1 tr in each of next 2 tr, 1 dc in each of next 2 dc, 1 hdc in next hdc, 1 sc in next sc, rep from * 3 times more to last 7 sts, ch 2, sk 2, 1 sc in next sc, 1 hdc in next hdc, 1 dc in next 2 dc, 1 tr in top of tch, turn.

Row 5: Ch 1 with MC, sk first st, work 1 sc in each of next 4 sts, inserting hook from front of work, 1 sc in each of 2 free sc three rows below, * 1 sc in each of next 10 sts, 2 sc three rows below, rep from * 3 times more, sc in each of last 4 sts, 1 sc in top of tch, turn.

Row 6: Ch 1, sk first st, work 1 sc in each st to end, 1 sc in top of tch, turn.

Row 7: Ch 1 with CC, do not sk first sc, * work 1 sc in first sc, 1 hdc in next sc, 1 dc in each of next 2 sc, 1 tr in each of next 2 sc, 1 dc in each of next 2 sc, 1 hdc in next sc, 1 sc in next sc, ch 2, sk 2 sc, rep from * 4 times more, omit ch 2 at end of last rep, turn.

Row 8: Ch 1, do not sk first st, * work 1 sc in first sc, 1 hdc in next hdc, 1 dc in each of next 2 dc, 1 tr in each of next 2 tr, 1 dc in each of next 2 dc, 1 hdc in next hdc, 1 sc in next sc, ch 2, sk 2, rep from * 4 times more, omit ch 2 at end of last rep, turn.

Row 9: Ch 1 with MC, do not sk first st, * work 1 sc in each of next 10 sts, * 1 sc in each of 2 free sc 3 rows below, rep from * 4 times more, turn.

Rep rows 2–9 one time more; fasten off. Mark center of one piece as back; skirt is worked in rnds from this point.

SKIRT
Rnd 1: Join MC at bottom of center back, work 30 sc along bottom of side of back, ch 2, work 60 sc along bottom of front, ch 2, work 30 sc along bottom of other side of back, join with Sl st—128 sts.

Rnd 2: Ch 3, work in dc, inc every 3 (2, 2) sts, work in ch 2 at each underarm, join with Sl st to top of beg ch 3—168 (190,190) sts.

Rnd 3: Ch 1, work 1 sc in each dc around, join with Sl st to beg ch 1.

Rnd 4: Ch 3, work 1 dc in each sc around, join with Sl st to top of beg ch 3.

Rep rnds 3 and 4 until skirt is 10½" (11", 11½") [26.7 (28, 29.3) cm]; fasten off.

SHOULDER STRAPS
Front RS facing you, starting 7 sts in from underarm, join CC, sc in each of next 8 sts, turn.

Row 1: Ch 1 (counts as sc), sk 1 st, sc in each of next 7 sts, turn.

Rep row 1 until 20 (22, 22) rows have been worked; fasten off.

Sk center 16 sts, join yarn, work second strap on next 8 sts to correspond.

Back, starting 7 sts in from underarm, join CC, work same as front for 22 (24, 24) rows, make buttonholes as foll:

* **Next row:** Work 1 sc in each of next 3 sts, ch 2, sk 2, sk next 3, turn.

Next row: Ch 1, sk 1, work 1 sc in each of next 2 sc, 2 sc in ch-2 sp, sc in next 3 sc, turn.

Work 6 rows of sc, rep from * two times more. After last buttonhole is made, work 2 rows of sc, dec 1 st each side of last row; fasten off.

WAIST TIE
Using double strand of MC, ch 175; fasten off.

FINISHING
1. Weave tie in and out of stitches at waistline. Tie at center front.
2. Sew side seams of yoke. Join MC at underarm, work 1 row sc around entire top edge, including straps, back to where you started; fasten off.
3. Weave in all loose ends, using tapestry needle.
4. Sew buttons on front straps to correspond to buttonholes.

Cool Stripes Sundress

Soft and adorable, this sweet little sundress is also a joy to crochet. It is made in one piece in rows worked sideways, with a striped border added at the bottom. The buttons at the shoulders, circled with pretty flowers, allow for toddler growth or to make extra room for layering over a shirt in cooler weather.

COOL STRIPES SUNDRESS

YARN

Lightweight cotton yarn

Shown: Grace by Patons, 100% cotton, 1.75 oz (50 g)/136 yd (125 m): Lilac #60321 (A), 2 (3, 3) skeins; Sweetpea (green) #60230 (B), 2 (2, 2) skeins; Sky (blue) #60130 (C), 2 (2, 2) skeins

HOOK

5/F (3.75 mm)

STITCHES USED

Single crochet

Single crochet through the back loop

Half double crochet

Double crochet

Double crochet through the back loop

Reverse single crochet

GAUGE

22 sc or 20 dc = 4" (10 cm)

NOTIONS

Tapestry needle

Eight buttons, 3/8" (1 cm) diameter

Hand-sewing needle

Thread

FINISHED SIZE

18 months (24 months, 2T)

Chest size: 20" (21", 22") [51 (53.5, 56) cm]

Vertical rows, worked through the back loop, are double crochet stitches for the skirt, changing to single crochet stitches for the bodice.

START AT BACK
Dress starts at center back seam and is worked vertically side to side. All vertical rows are worked tbl.

Foundation row: With A, ch 68 (70, 72). Starting in second ch from hook, work 1 sc in each of next 22 (23, 24) ch, 1 dc in each of next 44 (45, 46) ch, turn.

Row 1: Ch 3 (counts as dc), sk first dc, work 1 dc tbl in each of next 43 (44, 45), 1 sc tbl in each of next 22 (23, 24), 1 sc in top of tch, turn.

Row 2: Ch 1 (counts as sc), sk first sc, work 1 sc tbl in each of next 22 (23, 24), 1 dc tbl in each of next 43 (44, 45), 1 dc in top of tch, turn.

Rows 3, 5, 7, and 9: Rep row 1.

Rows 4, 6, 8, and 10: Rep row 2.

For 24 months, rep rows 1 and 2 one time more.
For 2T, rep rows 1 and 2 two times more.

At end of row 10 (12, 14), draw up lp with B; fasten off A.

LEFT SIDE
Row 1: With B, ch 3, sk first dc, work 1 dc tbl in each of next 43 (44, 45), 1 sc tbl in each of next 23 (24, 25), at end, ch an additional 11 (12, 13) for back shoulder tab, turn.

Row 2: Starting in second ch from hook, work 1 sc tbl of each new ch—10 (11, 12) sc—1 sc tbl in each established—23 (24, 25) sc—1 dc tbl in each established—43 (44, 45) dc—1 dc in top of tch, turn.

Single crochet stitches in rounds, worked horizontally, form the three-color lower border. One row of reverse single crochet adds a finishing touch.

Row 3: Ch 3 (counts as dc), sk first dc, work 1 dc tbl in each of next 43 (44, 45), 1 sc tbl in each of next 32 (34, 36), 1 sc in top of tch, turn.

Row 4: Ch 1 (counts as sc), sk first sc, work 1 sc tbl in each of next 31 (33, 35), 1 dc tbl in each of next 43 (44, 45), 1 dc in top of tch, turn.

Row 5: Ch 3 (counts as dc), sk first dc, work 1 dc tbl in each of next 43 (44, 45), 1 sc tbl in each of next 23 (24, 25). Make buttonholes on rem 10 (11, 12) as foll: work 1 sc in next 0 (1, 2) sc, * ch 1, sk 1, 1 sc in each of next 3 sc, rep from * one time more, ch 1, sk 1, 1 sc in top of tch, turn.

Row 6: Ch 1 (counts as sc), sk first sc, work 1 sc tbl in each of next 32 (34, 36), working tbl of each ch, 1 dc tbl in each of next 43 (44, 45),1 dc in top of tch, turn.

Row 7: Rep row 3.

Row 8: Rep row 4.

Row 9: Ch 3 (counts as dc), sk first dc, work 1 dc tbl in each of next 43 (44, 45). Shape armhole and front tab as foll: omit sc, ch 34 (36, 38), turn.

Row 10: Starting in second ch from hook, work 1 sc tbl in each of next 32 (34, 36) ch, 1 dc tbl in each of next 43 (44, 45), 1 dc in top of tch, turn.

Row 11: Ch 3 (counts as dc), sk first dc, work 1 dc tbl in each of next 43 (44, 45), 1 sc tbl in each of next 32 (34, 36), 1 sc in top of tch, turn.

Row 12: Ch 1 (counts as sc), sk first sc, work 1 sc tbl in each of next 32 (34, 36), 1 dc tbl in each of next 43 (44, 45), 1 dc in top of tch, turn.

Rows 13 and 15: Rep row 11.

Rows 14 and 16: Rep row 12; at end of row 16, pick up lp with A, fasten off B, turn.

FRONT PANEL
Row 1: With A, ch 3 (counts as dc), sk first dc, work 1 dc tbl in each of next 43 (44, 45), 1 sc tbl in each of next 17 (18, 19), turn.

Row 2: Ch 1 (counts as sc), sk first sc, work 1 sc tbl in each of next 16 (17, 18), 1 dc tbl in each of next 43 (44, 45), 1 dc in top of tch, turn.

Rows 3, 5, 7, 9, 11, 13, 15, 17, 19, 21, and 23: Rep row 1.

Rows 4, 6, 8, 10, 12, 14, 16, 18, 20, 22, and 24: Rep row 2.

For 24 months, rep rows 1 and 2 one time more.
For 2T, rep rows 1 and 2 two times more.

At end of last row, draw up lp with C, fasten off A, turn.

RIGHT SIDE AND BACK
With C, complete as for first side panel, reversing shaping and buttonholes. At end of this panel, draw up lp with A, fasten off C, and complete back as first color panel, reversing shaping.

TOP TRIM
Sew shoulder seams. Sew back seam up to sc rows.

Row 1: With A, RS facing you, starting at left top back opening, work 1 row sc along back neck, cont along entire edge, including tabs and armholes, 3 sc in last st at top right, cont sc down back opening, up other side, at top of opening, ch 6 for button lp, 1 sc in same st, do not turn.

Row 2: Work 1 sc in each sc just worked, except for back opening. When you are back to top of back opening, do not turn.

Row 3: Work 1 row rev sc on all sc except back opening; fasten off.

BOTTOM BORDER
Rnd 1: With C, starting at center back, work 1 row sc all around bottom, picking up 2 sc per row of dc, join with Sl st, do not turn.

Rnd 2: Ch 2, work 1 hdc in each st around, join with Sl st to top of beg ch 2, do not turn.

Rnds 3 and 4: Pick up lp with B, fasten off C, rep rnd 2.

Rnds 5 ,6 and 7: Pick of lp with A, fasten off B, rep rnd 2.

Rnd 8: With A, work 1 row rev sc; fasten off.

Two rows of single crochet and a row of reverse single crochet finish the bodice edges to perfection.

FLOWERS
Make 3.
Flowers can be slipped right over buttons or sewn on.

Foundation rnd: With B, ch 6, join with Sl st to form ring.

Rnd 1: Ch 1, work 10 sc in ring, join with Sl st.

Rnd 2: * Ch 2, work 3 dc in next st, ch 2, Sl st in next st, rep from * 4 times more, join with Sl st; fasten off—5 petals.

Dainty flowers can be buttoned directly over the tab buttons or sewn separately to the dress.

FINISHING
1. Weave in ends, using tapestry needle.
2. Sew buttons on front straps to correspond to buttonholes.
3. Attach flowers over buttons.

Cool Stripes Doll Dress

Make a little girl very happy with a doll's dress to match her own. Just like the sundress on page 36, this dress is crocheted vertically with a horizontal striped border.

START AT BACK

Dress starts at center back seam and is worked vertically side to side. All vertical rows are worked tbl.

Foundation row: With A, ch 43. Starting in second ch from hook, work 1 sc in each of next 14 ch, 1 dc in each of next 27 ch, turn.

Row 1: Ch 3 (counts as dc), sk first dc, work 1 dc tbl in each of next 26,
1 sc tbl in each of next 13, 1 sc in top of tch, turn.

Row 2: Ch 1 (counts as sc), sk first sc, work 1 sc tbl in each of next 13, 1 dc tbl in each of next 26, 1 dc in top of tch, turn.

Rows 3, 5, and 7: Rep row 1.

Rows 4, 6, and 8: Rep row 2. At end of row 8, draw up lp with B; fasten off A.

LEFT SIDE

Rows 9, 11, and 13: With B, rep row 1.

Rows 10, 12, and 14: Rep row 2.

Row 15: Ch 3 (counts as dc), sk first dc, work 1 dc tbl in each of next 26, omit sc, ch 16 (for armhole), turn.

Row 16: Starting in second ch from hook, work 1 sc tbl in each of next 14 ch, 1 dc tbl in each of next 26, 1 dc in top of tch, turn.

Rows 17 and 19: Rep row 1.

Rows 18 and 20: Rep row 2, pick up lp with A, fasten off B, turn.

Rows 21 and 23: With A, rep row 1.

Rows 22 and 24: Rep row 2.

SHAPE NECK

Row 25: Ch 3 (counts as dc), sk first dc, work 1 dc tbl in each of next 26, 1 sc tbl in each of next 10, turn.

Row 26: Ch 1 (counts as sc), sk first sc, work 1 sc tbl in each of next 9, 1 dc tbl in each of next 26, 1 dc in top of tch, turn.

Rows 27, 29, and 31: Rep row 25.

Rows 28, 30, and 32: Rep row 26.

Row 33: Ch 3 (counts as dc), sk first dc, work 1 dc tbl in each of next 26, 1 sc tbl in each of next 10, ch 6, turn.

COOL STRIPES DOLL DRESS

YARN

Lightweight cotton yarn

Shown: Grace by Patons, 100% cotton, 1.75 oz (50 g)/136 yd (125 m): Lilac #60321 (A), 1 skein; Sweetpea (green) #60230 (B), 1 skein; Sky (blue) #60130 (C), 1 skein

HOOK

5/F (3.75 mm)

STITCHES USED

Single crochet

Single crochet through the back loop

Half double crochet

Double crochet

Double crochet through the back loop

Reverse single crochet

GAUGE

22 sc or 20 dc = 4" (10 cm)

NOTIONS

Tapestry needle

Three buttons, 3/8" (1 cm) diameter

Hand-sewing needle

Thread

FINISHED SIZE

To fit dolls 17" to 19" (43 to 48.5 cm) tall

Row 34: Starting in second ch from hook, work 1 sc tbl in each of 5 ch, 1 sc tbl in each of next 10, 1 dc tbl in each of next 26, 1 dc in top of tch, turn.

Row 35: Ch 3 (counts as dc), sk first dc, work 1 dc tbl in each of next 26, 1 sc tbl in each of next 14, 1 sc in top of tch, turn.

Row 36: Ch 1 (counts as sc), work 1 sc tbl in each of next 14, 1 dc tbl in each of next 26, 1 dc in top of tch, pick up lp with C, fasten off A, turn.

RIGHT SIDE AND BACK
Rows 37, 39, and 41: With C, rep row 35.

Rows 38, 40, and 42: Rep row 36.

Row 43: Ch 3 (counts as dc), sk first dc, work 1 dc tbl in each of next 26, omit sc, ch 16, turn.

Row 44: Starting in second ch from hook, work 1 sc tbl in each of next 15 ch, 1 dc tbl in each of next 26, 1 dc in top of tch, turn.

Rows 45 and 47: Rep row 43.

Rows 46 and 48: Rep row 44, pull up lp with A, fasten off C, turn.

Rows 49, 51, 53, and 55: With A, rep row 43.

Rows 50, 52, 54, and 56: Rep row 44; fasten off.

TOP TRIM
Sew back seam, leaving 3½" (9 cm) from neck open. Sew shoulder seams. With A, starting at top of right back opening, work 20 sc along right back opening, 8 sc on left back opening, * ch 4, 4 sc, rep from * once, ch 4, 1 sc in last st, cont sc all around neck edge back to where you started, do not turn. Work 1 row rev sc around neck edge only; fasten off.

BOTTOM BORDER
Rnd 1: With C, work 1 row sc all around bottom, join with Sl st, do not turn.

Rnd 2: Ch 2, work 1 hdc in each st around, join with Sl st to top of beg ch 2, do not turn.

Rnd 3 and 4: Pick up lp with B, fasten off C, rep rnd 2.

Rnd 5: Pick up lp with A, fasten off B, rep rnd 2.

Rnd 6: With A, work 1 row rev sc; fasten off.

Three-button closure at the back makes it easy to dress dolly.

FLOWER
Make 3.

Foundation rnd: With B, ch 4, join with Sl st to form ring.

Rnd 1: Ch 1, work 10 sc in ring, join with Sl st.

Rnd 2: * Ch 1, work 3 hdc in next st, ch 1, Sl st in next st, rep from * 4 times more, join with Sl st; fasten off—5 petals.

FINISHING
1. Weave in ends, using tapestry needle.
2. Sew buttons on back opening to correspond to buttonholes.
3. Sew flowers to right shoulder.

Easy, Breezy Sleeveless Dress

This little A-line jumper is quick and easy to make. It can be worn as a sleeveless dress or paired with a T-shirt. Buttoned shoulder tabs can be adjusted as the child grows or to make room for a shirt.

EASY, BREEZY SLEEVELESS DRESS

YARN
Lightweight acrylic yarn

Shown: Astra by Patons, 100% acrylic, 1.75 oz (50 g)/133 yd (122 m): Medium Blue #02774 (MC), 3 (3, 4) skeins; White #02751 (A), 1 skein; Spring Green #2911 (B), 1 skein

HOOK
8/H (5 mm)

STITCHES USED
Single crochet

Double crochet

GAUGE
15 sc = 4" (10 cm)

NOTIONS
Tapestry needle

Four buttons, ½" (1.3 cm) diameter

Hand-sewing needle

Thread

FINISHED SIZE
18 months (24 months, 2T)

Chest size: 21" (22", 23") [53.5 (56, 58.5) cm]

BACK

Foundation row: With MC, ch 61 (63, 65). Starting in second ch from hook, work 1 sc in each ch across, turn—60 (62, 64) sts.

Row 1: Ch 3 (counts as dc), sk first st, work 1 dc in each st across, 1 dc in top of tch, turn.

Row 2: Ch 1, sk first st, work 1 sc in each st across, 1 sc in top of tch, turn.

Rep rows 1 and 2 until piece is 1½" (2", 2½") [3.8 (5, 6.5) cm], ending with dc row, turn.

First dec row: Ch 1, sk first st, sc2tog (dec made), work 1 sc in each of next 13 (14, 15) sts, sc2tog, 1 sc in each of next 2 sts, sc2tog, 1 sc in each of next 16 sts, sc2tog, 1 sc in each of next 2 sts, sc2tog, 1 sc in each of next 13 (14, 15) sts, sc2tog, 1 sc in top of tch, turn—54 (56, 58) sts.

Rep rows 1 and 2 until piece is 5½" (6", 6½") [14 (15, 16.3) cm] from beg, ending with dc row, turn.

Second dec row: Ch 1, sk first st, sc2tog, work 1 sc in each of next 11 (12, 13) sts, sc2tog, 1 sc in each of next 2 sts, sc2tog, 1 sc in each of next 14 sts, sc2tog, 1 sc in each of next 2 sts, sc2tog, 1 sc in each of next 11 (12, 13) sts, sc2tog, 1 sc in top of tch, turn—48 (50, 52) sts.

Rep rows 1 and 2 until piece is 8½" (9", 9½") [21.8 (23, 24.3) cm] from beg, ending with dc row, turn.

Third dec row: Ch 1, sk first st, sc2tog, work 1 sc in each of next 9 (10, 11) sts, sc2tog, 1 sc in each of next 2 sts, sc2tog, 1 sc in each of next 12 sts, sc2tog, 1 sc in each of next 2 sts, sc2tog, 1 sc in each of next 9 (10, 11) sts, sc2tog, 1 sc in top of tch, turn—42 (44, 46) sts.

Rep rows 1 and 2 until piece is 10½" (11", 11½") [26.7 (28, 29.3) cm] from beg, ending with dc row, turn.

Fourth dec row: Ch 1, sk first st, sc2tog, work 1 sc in each of next 7 (8, 9) sts, sc2tog, 1 sc in each of next 2 sts, sc2tog, 1 sc in each of next 10 sts, sc2tog, 1 sc in each of next 2 sts, sc2tog, 1 sc in each of next 7 (8, 9) sts, sc2tog, 1 sc in top of tch, turn—36 (38, 40) sts.

Rep rows 1 and 2 until piece is 11½" (12", 12½") [29.3 (30.5, 31.8) cm] from beg, ending with dc row, turn.

Shape armholes as foll: Sl st over 4 sts, work sc to within 4 sts of other side, turn—28 (30, 32) sts. Keeping patt as established, dec 1 st on each arm side in every row twice (to dec on dc row, dc2tog)—24 (26, 28) sts. Work even until armhole is 4" (4½", 5") [10 (11.5, 12.7) cm].

The entire dress is made by alternating rows of single and double crochet stitches. Single rows of single crochet stitches in each of two contrasting colors make a nice edging for the neckline and armholes.

Shape neck as foll: work across 9 sts, ch 1, turn. Dec 1 st on neck edge in every row twice. Work even on rem 7 sts until armhole is 6½" (7", 7½") [16.3 (18, 19.3) cm], fasten off. Sk center 6 (8, 10) sts, join yarn at neck edge, work rem 9 sts to correspond to other side; fasten off.

FRONT

Work same as back, except start neck shaping when armhole is 3" (3½", 4") [7.5 (9, 10) cm].

FINISHING

1. Sew side seams and weave in ends, using tapestry needle.
2. Using A and B, work 1 row sc in each color around entire upper edge, including straps.
3. Sew 2 buttons on each front tab. Buttonholes are not necessary, as dc rows are loose enough for buttons to fit through.

Easy, Breezy Cropped Jacket

This darling cropped jacket is the perfect companion to the sleeveless dress on page 46, but you can hook one up in any color combination you choose. With simple shaping and a one-piece body, the jacket goes together very quickly.

EASY, BREEZY CROPPED JACKET

YARN

Lightweight acrylic yarn

Shown: Astra by Patons, 100% acrylic, 1.75 oz (50 g)/133 yd (122 m): Medium Blue #02774 (MC), 3 (3, 4) skeins; White #02751 (A), 1 skein; Spring Green #2911 (B), 1 skein

HOOK

8/H (5 mm)

STITCHES USED

Single crochet
Double crochet

GAUGE

15 sc = 4" (10 cm)

Border pattern will pull in slightly.

NOTIONS

Tapestry needle
One button, 3/8" (1 cm) diameter
Hand-sewing needle
Thread

FINISHED SIZE

18 months (24 months, 2T)

Chest size: 26" (28", 30") [66 (71, 76) cm]

Intricate-looking, three-color border works up quickly with single crochet stitches in chain spaces.

BODY
Worked in one piece. While working border, carry yarn up sides.

Foundation row: With A, ch 97 (105, 113). Starting in second ch from hook, work 1 sc in each ch across, turn, do not fasten off A—96 (104, 112) sts. Pick up lp with B and ch 1, turn.

Row 1: Sk first st, work 1 sc in next st, * ch 1, sk next st, 1 sc in next st, rep from * across, end 1 sc in tch, pick up lp with MC, do not fasten off B, turn.

Row 2: Do not sk first st, work 1 sc in first st, * ch 1, sk next st, 1 sc in next ch-1 sp, rep from * across, end ch 1, sk 1 st, 1 sc in top of tch, pick up lp with A and ch 1, do not fasten off MC, turn.

Row 3: Work 1 sc in first st, * 1 sc in ch-1 sp, ch 1, sk 1 st, rep from * across, end 1 sc in top of tch, do not fasten off A, pick up lp with B, ch 1, turn.

Row 4: Rep row 3, do not fasten off B, pick up lp with MC, ch 1, turn.

Row 5: Rep row 3, do not fasten off MC, pick up lp with A, ch 1, turn.

Row 6: Rep row 3, fasten off A, pick up lp with B, ch 1, turn.

Row 7: Rep row 3, fasten off B, pick up lp with MC, ch 1, turn.

Row 8: Rep row 3, do not fasten off MC, turn.

Row 9: Ch 3 (counts as dc), sk first st, * work 1 dc in next ch-1 sp, 1 dc in next st, rep from * across, end 1 dc in tch, turn—96 (104, 112) dc.

Row 10: Ch 1, sk first st, work 1 sc in each st across, 1 sc in top of tch, turn—96 (104, 112) sc.

Row 11: Ch 3, sk first st, work 1 dc in each st across, 1 dc in top of tch, turn.

Rep rows 10 and 11 until piece is 5" (5½", 6") [12.7 (14, 15) cm] from the beg, ending with dc row, turn.

Left front: Work in sc across 22 (23, 25) sts, turn. Ch 3, sk first st, work 1 dc in each st across. Working on these 22 (23, 25) sts only, cont in patt until 3" (3½", 4") [7.5 (9, 10) cm] from underarm, end at neck edge. Sl st over 8 (8, 10) sts, finish row. Cont in patt on these 14 (15, 15) sts, dec 1 st on neck edge in every row twice. Work patt on rem 12 (13, 13) sts until armhole is 5" (5½", 6") [12.7 (14, 15) cm]; fasten off.

Back section: Sk 4 (6, 6) sts for underarm, join yarn, work patt on next 44 (46, 50) sts, ch 1, turn. Cont patt on these 44 (46, 50) sts only, until armholes are 5" (5½", 6") [12.7 (14, 15) cm]; fasten off.

Right front: Sk 4 (6, 6) sts for underarm, join yarn, and work rem 22 (23, 25) sts. Cont to work patt on 22 (23, 25) sts until 3" (3½", 4") [7.5 (9, 10) cm] from underarm, end at arm side. Work 14 (15, 15) sts, leave rem 8 (8, 10) sts not worked, ch 1, turn. Dec 1 st on neck edge in every row twice. Work patt on rem 12 (13, 13) sts until armhole is 5" (5½", 6") [12.7 (14, 15) cm]; fasten off.

SLEEVES
Make 2.

Ch 29 (31, 33). Work foundation and first 8 rows same as body.

Row 9: Ch 3, work 1 dc in first st, * 1 dc in next ch-1 sp, 1 dc in next st, rep from * across, end 2 dc in last st, 1 dc in top of tch, turn—30 (32, 34) dc.

Cont in patt as established (1 row sc, 1 row dc), inc 1 st each side every 1½" (3.8 cm) 4 times more—38 (40, 42) sts.

Work even until sleeve is 8½" (9", 9½") [21.8 (23, 24.3) cm] from beg, fasten off.

FINISHING
1. Weave in ends, using tapestry needle.
2. Sew shoulder seams.
3. Fold each sleeve in half, center and pin at shoulder seam, sew in place.
4. Sew underarm seams.
5. Work border (see below).
6. Sew on button.

FRONT/NECK BORDER
With B, starting at bottom right corner, RS facing you, work in sc to neck edge, 3 sc in last st, cont sc around neck edge, 3 sc in top st to turn corner, cont down left side to bottom; fasten off.

Join A at bottom of right front, work sc in each st to top, ch 6 for button lp, cont around neck, down front edge; fasten off.

Color Block Pullover

By changing the color combination, this pullover can be a great choice for either a boy or a girl. This sweater is soft, warm, and toasty, made in a machine washable acrylic/wool blend. Button closures at the shoulders make it easy to get on and off.

COLOR BLOCK PULLOVER

YARN
Medium-weight acrylic/wool yarn

Shown: Encore by Plymouth, 75% acrylic/25% wool, 3.5 oz (100 g)/200 yd (184 m): Green #3335 (A), 1 (1, 1) skein; Turquoise #234 (B), 1 (1, 2) skein; Lavender #1308 (C), 1 (1, 1) skein

HOOK
10/J (6 mm)

STITCHES USED
Single crochet
Double crochet
Popcorn stitch

GAUGE
12 sc = 4" (10 cm)

NOTIONS
Tapestry needle
Six buttons, ¾" (2 cm) diameter
Hand-sewing needle
Thread

FINISHED SIZE
18 months (24 months, 2T)
Chest size: 25" (26", 27") [63.5 (66, 68.5) cm]

STITCH PATTERN
Popcorn stitch: [Yo, pick up lp] 3 times in next st, yo through all 7 lps at once.

BACK
Foundation row: With A, ch 39 (41, 43). Starting in second ch from hook (counts as sc), * work 1 dc in next ch, 1 sc in next ch, rep from * across, turn—38 (40, 42) sts.

Row 1: Ch 3 (counts as dc), sk first sc, * work 1 sc in next dc, 1 dc in next sc, rep from * 17 (18, 19) times more, end 1 sc in tch, turn—38 (40, 42) sts.

Rep row 1 until piece is 7½" (8", 8½") [19.3 (20.5, 21.8) cm] from beg. Do not fasten off A, pick up lp with B, turn.

Next row: Ch 1 (counts as sc), sk first st, work 1 sc in each of next 36 (38, 40) sts, 1 sc in tch, turn—38 (40, 42) sts.

Next row: Ch 1 (counts as sc), sk first st, work 1 sc in each of next 36 (38, 40) sts, 1 sc in tch, pick up lp with A, do not fasten off B, turn.

Pc row: Ch 1 (counts as sc), sk first st, work 1 sc in each of next 4 (5, 6) sts, * pc in next st, 1 sc in each of next 2 sts, rep from * 9 times more (10 pc in all), end with 1 sc in last 2 (3, 4) sts, 1 sc in tch, fasten off A, do not turn.

Go back to beg of pc row, pick up B, rep 2 rows of sc in B, pull up lp with C in last st, fasten off B, turn.

Note: Color blocks of top back are worked separately and sewn tog. Shape armhole as foll: using C, Sl st over 2 sts, work same patt as beg of back on next 14 (15, 16) sts, turn.

Working on these 14, (15, 16) sts only, cont until armhole is 5½" (6", 6½") [14 (15, 16.3) cm], ending at arm side.

Shape neck as foll: Sl st over 2 sts, cont patt on next 10 (11, 12) sts (leave rem sts not worked), work 2 more rows on 10 (11, 12) sts, turn.

Make button lps as foll: ch 1 (does not count as first st), work 1 sc in each of next 1 (2, 3) sts, * ch 2, sk 1 st, 1 sc in next st, rep from * two times more; fasten off C.

Join B in next st to left of first color block, work patt as established over next 20 (21, 22) sts, leaving 2 sts at end not worked, turn.

Work on these 20 (21, 22) to correspond to other side, reversing neck shaping and buttonhole placement.

FRONT
Work same as back, until 2 rows after pc row.

On RS, join B, Sl st over 2 sts, work patt on next 20 (21, 22), turn. Cont to

Alternating single and double crochet stitches in each row form a soft, pebbly surface. Popcorn stitch row is preceded and followed by two rows of single crochet.

work patt as established on these 20 (21, 22) sts until armhole is 4½" (5", 5½") [11.5 (12.7, 14) cm], ending at arm side.

Work across next 10 (11, 12) sts, leaving 10 (10, 10) not worked, turn. Cont to work patt as established on 10 (11, 12) until armhole is 5½" (6", 6½") [14 (15, 16.3) cm]; fasten off B.

Join C in next st to left of first color block, work patt on next 14 (15, 16) sts, leaving 2 sts at arm side not worked (for armhole). Cont to work patt as established on these 14 (15, 16) sts until same as other side to neck shaping, Sl st over 4 sts, cont patt on rem 10 (11, 12) until same as other side to shoulder; fasten off C.

SLEEVES
Make 1 in B and 1 in C.

Ch 25 (27, 29). Work in same patt as back, inc 1 st each side every 1½" (3.8 cm) 5 times, being sure to keep patt as sts inc—34 (36, 38) sts.

Work even in patt until sleeve is 10½" (11", 11½") [26.7 (28, 29.3) cm] from beg; fasten off.

FINISHING
1. Weave in ends, using tapestry needle.
2. Sew seams, joining top pieces of front and backs to each other.
3. Sew shoulder seams (2 stitches on each shoulder form shoulder seam).
4. Fold each sleeve in half, center and pin at shoulder seam, and sew in place.
5. Sew underarm seams.
6. Sew on buttons to correspond to buttonholes.

Summer Fun Vest

Your little guy will really win the vote wearing his red, white, and blue vest. The star buttons add a fun touch. Quick and easy to make, and great for gift giving, too, the vest can also be made in other color schemes with playful buttons.

SUMMER FUN VEST

YARN

Lightweight acrylic yarn

Shown: Astra by Patons, 100% acrylic, 1.75 oz (50 g)/178 yd (163 m): Electric Blue #02733 (A), 1 (1, 2) skein; White #02751 (B), 1 skein; Crayon Red #246008 (C), 1 skein

HOOK

10/J (6 mm)

STITCH USED

Single crochet

GAUGE

12 sc = 4" (10 cm)

NOTIONS

Tapestry needle
Five star buttons
Hand-sewing needle
Thread

FINISHED SIZE

18 months (24 months, 2T)

Chest size: 21" (22", 23") [53.5 (56, 58.5) cm]

Vest is worked entirely in single crochet, alternating red and white for each row on the right side. Three-color border around the armholes and front/neck includes four buttonholes.

BACK

Foundation row: With A, ch 35 (37, 39). Starting in second ch from hook, work 1 sc in each ch across, turn—34 (36, 38) sts.

Row 1 (RS): Ch 1 (counts as sc), sk first st, work 1 sc in each of next 32 (34, 36) sts, 1 sc in top of tch, turn—34 (36, 38) sts.

Rep row 1 with A until piece is 5½" (6", 6½") [14 (15, 16.3) cm] from beg, ending on WS row.

Shape armhole as foll: Sl st over 6 sts, work to within 6 sts of other side, turn. Work 1 more row sc on 22 (24, 26) sts, pull up lp with C, fasten off A, turn.

With C, rep row 1 until armhole is 5½" (6", 6½") [14 (15, 16.3) cm]; fasten off.

RIGHT FRONT

Worked with colors B and C, alternating every 2 rows. Do not fasten off yarn each time, but carry loosely up front edge, to be worked over when border is done.

Foundation row: With C, ch 18 (19, 20). Starting in second ch from hook, work 1 sc in each ch across, turn—17 (18, 19) sts.

Row 1 (RS): Ch 1 (counts as sc), sk first st, work 1 sc in each of next 15 (16, 17) sts, 1 sc in top of tch, turn—17 (18, 19) sts.

Row 2: Pick up lp with B, rep row 1.

Row 3: Rep row 2.

Row 4: Pick up lp with C, rep row 1.

Cont to alternate B and C every 2 rows until piece is 5½" (6", 6½") [14 (15, 16.3) cm], ending with WS row at front edge. Pick up next color, work across 11 (12, 13) sts, leave rem 6 sts at arm side not worked, turn. Work 1 row back to front edge.

Cont in striping patt, and at the same time, dec 1 st at neck edge on next and every fourth row until 6 (6, 7) sts rem. Work even until armhole is 5½" (6", 6½") [14 (15, 16.3) cm]; fasten off.

LEFT FRONT
Using A only, work same as right front to armhole. At armhole, end at arm side instead of front edge, Sl st over 6 sts, work rem 11 (12, 13), cont shaping neck edge as right front; fasten off.

FINISHING
1. Weave in ends, using tapestry needle.
2. Sew shoulder seams, sew underarm seams.
3. Work border (see below).
4. Sew on buttons to correspond to buttonholes.

FRONT/NECK BORDER
Row 1: With C, starting at bottom right edge, work in sc along row ends, 24 (25, 26) sts to beg of V-neck shaping, 22 (23, 24) sts along right side of V, 12 (13, 14) sts along back of neck, 22 (23, 24) sts along left side of V, 24 (25, 26) sts along left front to bottom; fasten off C.

Row 2: Join B at bottom right, work as row 1 to end of V on left front. Work buttonholes as foll: * ch 3, sk 2 sts, work 1 sc in each of next 5 sts, rep from * 2 times more, ch 3, sk 2 sts, 1 sc in each of last 1 (2, 3) sts, fasten off B—4 buttonholes made.

Row 3: Join A at bottom right, work as row 1, making 2 sc in each ch-3 sp; fasten off.

ARMHOLE BORDER
Row 1: Join C at underarm seam, work 1 row sc along row ends all around armhole, pick up lp with B; fasten off C.

Row 2: Sc each st around, pick lp with A; fasten off B.

Row 3: Sc each st around; fasten off.

Cool Weather Cardigan

Perfect for early spring or the first cool days of fall, this lightweight wool cardigan can be made to suit a girl or a boy. Classic styling, rich colors, and an easy stitch equal a great little sweater.

COOL WEATHER CARDIGAN

YARN

Fine wool yarn

Shown: Baby Ull from Dale of Norway, 100% wool, 1.75 oz (50 g)/191 yd (175 m): #7436 (MC), 4 skeins; #6027 (CC), 1 skein

HOOKS

4/E (3.5 mm)

5/F (3.75 mm)

STITCHES USED

Single crochet

Single crochet through the back loop

GAUGE

18 sc = 4" (10 cm) using 5/F hook

NOTIONS

Tapestry needle

Five buttons, 5/8" (1.5 cm) diameter

Hand-sewing needle

Thread

FINISHED SIZE

18 months (24 months, 2T)

Chest size: 24" (26" 28") [61 (66, 71) cm]

BACK

Work ribbed borders first, then pick up sts along long edge of border (row ends) and cont for body of cardigan.

Foundation row: With MC and 4/E hook, ch 11. Work 1 sc in second ch from hook, 1 sc in each rem ch, turn—10 sts.

Row 1: Ch 1 (counts as sc), sk first st, work 1 sc tbl in each st, 1 sc in tch, turn.

Rep row 1 until 76 (80, 84) rows are worked; do not fasten off.

Working along row ends, ch 1 (counts as sc), sk first row end, work 1 sc in each of next 2 row ends, sk next row end, * 1 sc in each of next 3 row ends, sk next row end, rep from * 17 (18, 19) times more, 1 sc last row end—56 (60, 64) sts.

Change to 5/F hook, do not break MC, carry yarn loosely up sides for striping patt. Cont to work in sc, 2 rows CC, 2 rows MC, 2 rows CC, fasten off CC, cont to work in sc with MC until piece is 8" (8½", 9") [20.5 (21.8, 23) cm] from beg.

Shape armholes as foll: Sl st over 3 (3, 3) sts, work to within 3 (3, 3) sts of other side, ch 1, turn.

Cont to work on rem 50 (54, 58) sts until armhole is 4½" (5", 5½") [11.5 (12.7, 14) cm], ending with WS row. Work over 15 (16, 17) sts, ch 1, turn.

Dec neck edge every row twice, work even until armhole is 5½" (6", 6½") [14 (15, 16.3) cm], fasten off. Sk center 20 (22, 24) sts, join yarn, work 15 (16, 17) of other side to correspond; fasten off.

LEFT FRONT

With 4/E hook and MC, work band same as back for 38 (40, 42) rows, ch 1, work along top of border as foll: ch 1 (counts as sc), sk first row end, work 1 sc in each of next 2 (2, 3) row ends, * sk next row end, 1 sc in each of next 3 row ends, rep from * 7 (8, 8) times more, end sk 1 row end, 1 sc in last (last, 2 rem) row ends—28 (30, 32) sts.

Work as back to armhole, ending at arm side, Sl st over 3 (3, 3) sts, work rem 25 (27, 29) until armhole is 4" (4½", 5") [10 (11.5, 12.7) cm], ending at arm side.

Shape neck as foll: work in patt to within 8 sts of front edge, ch 1, turn. Working on rem 17 (19, 21), dec 1 st on neck edge every row 2 times. Work even on rem 15, (17, 19) sts until armhole is 5½" (6", 6½") [14 (15, 16.3) cm]; fasten off.

RIGHT FRONT

Work same as left front, reversing all shaping.

Sweater is worked entirely in single crochet with stripes of contrasting color at bottom of body and sleeves. Ribbed border is crocheted sideways with all single crochet stitches worked into the back loop.

SLEEVES

With 4/E hook and MC, work border same as back for 42 (44, 46) rows, ch 1, sc along top of border, picking up 1 st in each row end—42 (44, 46) sts.

Change to 5/F hook, work striping patt same as back, on last row, inc 1 st each side—44 (46, 48) sts. Cont working in sc, inc 1 st each side every sixth row 4 times more—52 (54, 56) sts.

Work even until sleeve is 9½" (10", 10½") [24.3 (25.5, 26.7) cm] from beg; fasten off.

FINISHING

1. Sew shoulder seams. Weave in ends, using tapestry needle.
2. Fold each sleeve in half, center and pin at shoulder seam, sew in place.
3. Sew underarm seams.
4. Work border (see below).
5. Sew on buttons to correspond to buttonholes.

FRONT/NECK BORDER

Row 1: Using 4/E hook and CC, RS facing you, join yarn at bottom right front. Sc along row ends as foll: 9 sc in border, 45 (47, 49) sc to neck edge, 3 sc in last st to turn corner, 12 (13, 14) sc along top of right front, 20 (22, 24) sc along back of neck, 12 (13, 14) sc along top of left front, 3 sc in last st to turn corner, 45 (47, 49) sc to top of border, 9 sc in border, turn.

Row 2: Work 1 sc in each st, making 3 sc in each corner st, pick up lp with MC in last st, do not fasten off CC, turn.

Row 3: With MC, work 1 sc in each st, 3 sc in each corner, work to top of left front, make buttonholes as foll: work 3 sc in corner st, ch 3, sk 2 (first buttonhole), 1 sc in each of next 11 sts, rep from * 3 times more, ch 3, sk 2, 1 sc in each st to end, turn—5 buttonholes.

Row 4: Ch 1, work 1 sc in each st, 2 sc in each buttonhole sp, 3 sc to turn corners, pull up lp with CC in last st; fasten off MC.

Rows 5 and 6: With CC, 1 sc in each st, 3 sc in each corner; fasten off.

Flower Border Cardigan

Pretty flowers all in a row add precious detail to this classic cardigan. The flower row stitch pattern, also used for the Pretty Posies Dress (page 8) and Hat (page 14), is a little challenging, but fun to do once you get the idea.

FLOWER BORDER CARDIGAN

YARN
Medium-weight acrylic/wool yarn

Shown: Encore by Plymouth, 75% acrylic/25% wool, 3.5 oz (100 g)/200 yd (184 m): Pale Yellow #896 (MC), 2 skeins; Lilac #233 (A), 1 skein; Green #3335 (B), 1 skein

HOOKS
8/H (5 mm)
9/I (5.5 mm)

STITCHES USED
Single crochet
Double crochet

GAUGE
14 sc = 4" (10 cm) using 9/I hook

NOTIONS
Tapestry needle
Five buttons, ⅝" (1.5 cm) diameter
Hand-sewing needle
Thread

FINISHED SIZE
18 months (24 months, 2T)
Chest size: 23" (24", 25") 58.5 (61, 63.5) cm]

Medium-weight acrylic/wool blend yarn in single crochet makes a warm sweater.

BODY

Body of cardigan is worked in one piece to armholes, then divided for front and back sections.

Foundation row: With 9/I hook and MC, ch 80 (84, 88). Starting in second ch from hook, work 1 sc in each ch, turn—79 (83, 87) sc.

Row 1: Ch 1 (counts as sc), sk first sc, work 1 sc in next sc, * ch 1, sk 1, rep from * across, end 1 sc in next sc, 1 sc in top of tch, turn; do not fasten off MC.

Row 2: Pick up lp with A, ch 2 (counts as sc and ch 1), sk next sc, work 1 sc in next ch-1 sp, * ch 1, sk next sc, 1 sc in next ch-1 sp, rep from * across, end ch 1, sk 1, 1 sc in top of tch, do not fasten off A, turn.

Row 3: Pick up lp with B, ch 1, work 1 sc in ch-1 sp, * ch 1, sk 1, 1 sc in next ch-1 sp, rep from * across, end 1 sc in top of tch, turn.

Rep rows 1 and 2, foll color sequence (MC, A, B) one time more, do not fasten off A and B—carry loosely up sides.

Next row: With MC, ch 1, sk first sc, work 1 sc in each sc and each ch-1 sp across, 1 sc in top of tch, turn—79 (83, 87) sc.

Beg flower patt as foll:

Row 1: With B, ch 1, sk first sc, work 1 sc in each of next 3 (5, 7) sc, * [in next sc (sc, ch 8) 3 times, sc], 1 sc in each of next 9 sc, rep from * 7 times more, end 1 sc in each of next 3 (5, 7) sc, 1 sc in top of tch, turn. Pull up lp with A, fasten off B.

Row 2: Ch 1 (counts as sc), sk first sc, work 1 sc in each of next 3 (5, 7) sc, * ch 1, sk ch lps, 1 sc in each of next 9 sc, rep from * across, end 1 sc in each of next 3 (5, 7) sc, 1 sc in top of tch, turn.

Row 3: Ch 1 (counts as sc), sk first sc, work 1 sc in each of next 0 (2, 4) sc, * 1 sc through right lp and into next sc, 1 sc in each of next 2 sc, 1 sc in ch-1 sp, 1 sc in each of next 2 sc, 1 sc through left lp and into next sc, 1 sc in each of next 3 sc, rep from * across, end 1 sc in each of next 0 (2, 4) sc, 1 sc in top of tch, turn.

Row 4: Ch 1, sk first sc, work 1 sc in each sc, 1 sc in top of tch, turn.

Row 5: Ch 1, sk first sc, work 1 sc in each of next 3 (5, 7) sc, * 6 dc through center lp and into next sc (flower bud made), 1 sc in each of next 9 sc, rep from * across, end 1 sc in each of next 3 (5, 7) sc, 1 sc in top of tch, turn.

Row 6: Ch 1 with MC (counts as sc), fasten off A, work 1 sc in each of next 3 (5, 7) sc, * ch 1, sk all dc, 1 sc in each of next 9 sc, rep from * across, end 1 sc in each of last 3 (5, 7) sc, 1 sc in top of tch, turn.

Row 7: Ch 1 (counts as sc), sk first sc, work 1 sc in each sc and in each ch-1 sp across, 1 sc in top of tch, turn.

Continuing with MC, work in sc on 79 (83, 87) sts until piece is 8" (8½", 9") [20.5 (21.8, 23) cm] from beg, ending on WS row.

RIGHT FRONT

Work in sc across 18 (19, 20) sts, ch 1, turn. Working on these 18 (19, 20) sts, work even until armhole is 3" (3½", 4") [7.5 (9, 10) cm], ending at neck edge. Sl st over 6 (6, 6) sts, ch 1, cont sc on rem 12 (13, 14) sts, dec 1 st at neck edge every row two times, work even on rem 10 (11, 12) sts until armhole is 5" (5½", 6") [12.7 (14, 15) cm]; fasten off.

Three loops of chain stitches, formed in the green base row, become leaves and a stem as they are caught into stitches in the following lavender rows.

BACK

Sk 4 sts at underarm, join yarn for back, work across 35 (37, 39) sts, ch 1, turn. Cont in sc for 4½" (5", 5½") [11.5 (12.7, 14) cm].

Shape back neck as foll: on the next row, work 10 (11, 12) sts, ch 1, turn. Work 1 more row on sts just worked; fasten off. Sk center 15 (15, 15) sts, join yarn, ch 1, work 2 rows sc on rem 10 (11, 12) sts; fasten off.

LEFT FRONT

Sk 4 sts at underarm, join yarn, work across 18 (19, 20) sts in sc until armhole is 3" (3½", 4") [7.5 (9, 10) cm], ending at arm side. Work across 12 (13, 14) sts, leave rem 6 sts not worked, turn. Complete dec as on right front; fasten off.

SLEEVES

Make 2.

With 8/H hook, ch 28 (28, 30). Work border same as back for 8 rows, fasten off A and B and cont sleeve in MC as foll:

Change to 9/I hook. On first MC row, inc 1 st each side and rep inc every 1¾" (4.5 cm) 4 (5, 5) times more—37 (39, 41) sc.

Work even until sleeve is 10" (10½", 11") [25.5 (26.7, 28) cm] from beg; fasten off.

FINISHING

1. Weave in ends, using tapestry needle.
2. Sew shoulder seams.
3. Fold each sleeve in half, center and pin at shoulder seam, sew in place.
4. Sew underarm seams.
5. Work front border (see below).
6. Sew on buttons to correspond to buttonholes.

Smaller hook used for the alternating color rows at the beginning of the sleeves makes these rows a little more snug.

Rows of single crochet in alternating colors form the neck border and buttonband.

FRONT BORDER

Row 1: With 8/H hook and B, starting at bottom right front, RS facing you, work 42 (44, 46) sc along front edge to top of right front, 3 sc in last st to turn corner, 11 (12, 13) sts along top of right front, 18 (20, 22) sts along back of neck, 11 (12, 13) sts along top of left front, 3 sc in last st to turn corner, 42 (44, 46) sts to bottom, turn.

Row 2: Ch 1, sk first st, work 1 sc in each st around, making 3 sc in each corner st, fasten off B, turn.

Row 3 (start of buttonholes): Pick up lp and ch 1 with A, sk first st, work 1 sc next 1 (2, 3) st, * ch 2, sk 2 sts, 1 sc in each of next 8 sts, rep from * 3 times more, ch 5, 1 sc in same st (this lp counts as fifth buttonhole and turns corner at same time. Cont around neck edge and down left front, turn.

Row 4: Ch 1, sk first st, work 1 sc in each st around, 2 sc in each ch-sp of buttonholes, fasten off A, turn.

Row 5: Pick up lp and ch 1 with MC, work 1 sc in each st around, 3 sc in each corner st, turn.

Row 6: Ch 1, Sl st in each st around, do not work 3 Sl st in corner st; fasten off.

Blue Cables Pullover

This comfy, loose-fitting pullover is suitable for a boy or girl. Big buttons at the shoulders make it easy to slip the sweater on or off. You'll enjoy working the cable pattern—it's easier than it looks.

BLUE CABLES PULLOVER

YARN

Medium-weight acrylic/wool yarn

Shown: Encore by Plymouth, 75% acrylic/25% wool, 3.5 oz (100 g)/200 yd (184 m): Medium Blue #4045, 3 skeins

HOOK

9/I (5.5 mm)

STITCHES USED

Single crochet

Front post double crochet

GAUGE

12 sc = 4" (10 cm)

NOTIONS

Tapestry needle

Six buttons, 5/8" (1.5 cm) diameter

Hand-sewing needle

Thread

FINISHED SIZE

18 months (24 months, 2T)

Chest size: 22" (24", 26") [56 (61, 66) cm]

Front post double crochet stitches form the cables on the front, back, and sleeves. Buttonhole tabs on the back shoulders overlap the front shoulders.

BACK

Foundation row: Ch 40 (42, 44). Starting in second ch from hook, work 1 sc in each ch across, turn—39 (41, 43) sc.

Row 1: Ch 1 (counts as sc), sk first sc, work 1 sc in each sc across, turn.

Row 2 and all even rows (WS): Ch 1, sk first sc, work 1 sc in each of next 37 (39, 41) sc, 1 sc in top of tch, turn.

Row 3: Beg cable as foll: ch 1, sk first sc, work 1 sc in each of next 8 (9, 10) sc, * FPdc around sc 2 rows below, sk sc behind FPdc, 1 sc in next sc, FPdc around sc 2 rows below, sk sc behind FPdc, 1 sc in each of next 6 sc, rep from * 2 times more, 1 sc in each of next 2 (3, 4) sc, 1 sc in top of tch, turn.

Row 5: Ch 1, sk first sc, work 1 sc in each of next 8 (9, 10) sc, * FPdc around post of next FPdc, sk sc behind FPdc, 1 sc in next sc, FPdc around post of next FPdc, sk sc behind FPdc, 1 sc in each of next 6 sc, rep from * 2 times more, 1 sc in each of next 2 (3, 4) sc, 1 sc in top of tch, turn.

Row 7: Ch 1, sk first sc, work 1 sc in each of next 8 (9, 10) sc, * sk over next FPdc and next sc, FPdc around next FPdc, 1 sc in sc bet 2 bars, FPdc back over FPdc that was skipped, 1 sc in each of next 6 sc, rep from * 2 times more, 1 sc in each of next 2 (3, 4) sc, 1 sc in top of tch, turn.

Row 9: Ch 1, sk first sc, work 1 sc in each of next 8 (9, 10) sc, * FPdc around next FPdc, sk sc behind FPdc, 1 sc in next sc, FPdc around next

FPdc, 1 sc in each of next 6 sc, rep from * 2 times more, 1 sc in each of next 2 (3, 4) sc, 1 sc in top of tch, turn.

Rep rows 4–9 until piece is 9½" (10", 10½") [24.3 (25.5, 26.7) cm] from beg.

Keeping patt as established, shape armholes as foll: Sl st over 4 sc, work to last 4 sc, turn. Work until armhole is 5½" (6", 6½") [14 (15, 16.3) cm], turn.

Work shoulder tabs as foll: ch 1, sk first sc, work sc in each of next 9 sc, turn.

Next row: Ch 1, sk first sc, work 1 sc in each sc, turn.

Next row: Ch 1, sk first sc, work 1 sc in next sc, ch 2, sk 1, 1 sc in each of next 2 sc, ch 2, sk 1, 1 sc in each of next 2 sc, ch 2, sk 1, 1 sc in last sc, turn—3 buttonholes made.

Next row: Work 1 sc in each sc and in each sp; fasten off.

Sk center 12 (13, 14) sc, work 10 sc on other side for other tab; fasten off.

FRONT
Work same as back until armhole is 4½" (5", 5½") [11.5 (12.7, 14) cm].

Left front: Work across 12 sc, turn. Sk first st, sc2tog next st, 1 sc in each st to end, turn—11 sc). Ch 1, sk first st, 1 sc in each of next 7 sts, sc2tog, 1 sc in tch—10 sc. Work even on rem 10 sts until armhole is 5½" (6", 6½") [14 (15, 16.3) cm]; fasten off.

Right front: Sk center 12 (13, 14) sc, join yarn and work rem 12 sc to correspond to left front.

SLEEVES
Make 2.

Foundation row: Ch 22 (24, 26). Starting in second ch from hook, work 1 sc in each st across, turn—21 (23, 25) sc.

Work in sc, keeping 3 sts in center in cable patt, and at same time, inc 1 st each side every 1½" (3.8 cm) 6 times. Work even on 33 (35, 37) sts until sleeve is 9½" (10", 10½") [24.3 (25.5, 26.7) cm] from beg; fasten off.

FINISHING
1. Weave in ends, using tapestry needle.
2. Sew shoulder seam ½" (1.3 cm) on each side.
3. Fold each sleeve in half, center and pin at shoulder seam, sew in place.
4. Sew underarm seams.
5. Sew on buttons.

Blue Cables Beanie

Hook a cabled hat to match the sweater on page 72. The hat is crocheted flat, then sewn together up the back. Playful curlicues stitched to the crown add a little fun.

HAT

Foundation row: Ch 57. Starting in second ch from hook, work 1 sc in each ch across, turn—56 sc.

Row 1: Ch 1 (counts as sc), sk first sc, work 1 sc in each sc across, turn.

Row 2 and all even rows (WS): Ch 1, sk first sc, work 1 sc in each of next 54 sc, 1 sc in top of tch, turn.

Row 3: Beg cable as foll: ch 1, sk first sc, work 1 sc in each of next 3 sc, * FPdc around sc 2 rows below, sk sc behind FPdc, 1 sc in next sc, FPdc around sc 2 rows below, sk sc behind FPdc, 1 sc in each of next 6 sc, rep from * 5 times more, 1 sc in each of next 3 sc, 1 sc in top of tch, turn.

Row 5: Ch 1, sk first sc, work 1 sc in each of next 3 sc, * FPdc around post of next FPdc, sk sc behind FPdc, 1 sc in next sc, FPdc around post of next FPdc, sk sc behind FPdc, 1 sc in each of next 6 sc, rep from * 5 times more, 1 sc in each of next 3 sc, 1 sc in top of tch, turn.

Row 7: Ch 1, sk first sc, work 1 sc in each of next 3 sc, * sk over next FPdc and next sc, FPdc around next FPdc, 1 sc in sc bet 2 bars, FPdc back over FPdc that was skipped, 1 sc in each of next 6 sc, rep from * 5 times more, 1 sc in each of next 3 sc, 1 sc in top of tch, turn.

Row 9: Ch 1, sk first sc, work 1 sc in each of next 3 sc, * FPdc around next FPdc, sk sc behind FPdc, 1 sc in next sc, FPdc around next FPdc, 1 sc in each of next 6 sc, rep from * 5 times more, 1 sc in each of next 3 sc, 1 sc in top of tch, turn.

Rep rows 4–9 until 5" (12.7 cm) from beg.

Beg dec: foll patt as established, sc2tog before and after each of 6 cables every other row 3 times. There will be 20 sts left after all dec are made.

Next row: Sc2tog across, fasten off, leaving a long tail for sewing. Gather the rem sts and pull tightly, then sew back seam, using tapestry needle. Weave in ends.

CURLICUES
Make 3.

Ch 25, work 2 sc in each ch; fasten off, leaving a tail for sewing. Stitch curlicues to top of hat.

BLUE CABLES BEANIE

YARN

Medium-weight acrylic/wool yarn

Shown: Encore by Plymouth, 75% acrylic/25% wool, 3.5 oz (100 g)/200 yd (184 m): Medium Blue #4045, 1 skein

HOOK

9/I (5.5 mm)

STITCHES USED

Single crochet

Single crochet two together

Front post double crochet

GAUGE

12 sc = 4" (10 cm)

NOTION

Tapestry needle

FINISHED SIZE

18" (46 cm) head circumference

Petite Shells Apricot Pullover

Cuddle your little girl in this roomy, warm, pullover sweater hooked entirely in an easy mini-shell pattern. Button loops close the shoulders so the sweater is easy to get on and off. The rolled sleeve cuff can be let down as she grows, and a little shell edging can be added for extra length.

PETITE SHELLS APRICOT PULLOVER

YARN

Lightweight acrylic yarn

Shown: Astra by Patons, 100% acrylic, 1.75 oz (50 g)/133 yd (122 m): Apricot #2731, 6 skeins

HOOKS

6/G (4 mm)

8/H (5 mm)

STITCHES USED

Single crochet

Half double crochet

Shell stitch

GAUGE

6 shells = 4" (10 cm) using 8/H hook

NOTIONS

Tapestry needle

Six buttons, ¾" (2 cm) diameter

Hand-sewing needle

Thread

FINISHED SIZE

18 months (24 months, 2T)

Chest size: 24" (25", 26") [61 (63.5, 66) cm]

BACK

Foundation row: With 8/H hook, ch 42 (44, 46). Starting in fourth ch from hook, * work [1 sc, ch 2, 1 sc] all in same ch (shell made), sk 1 ch, rep from * 17 (18, 19) times more, end sk 1 ch, 1 hdc in last ch, turn—18 (19, 20) shells.

Row 1: Ch 2, * work [1 sc, ch 2, 1 sc] in next ch-2 sp, rep from * 17 (18, 19) times more, end 1 hdc in tch, turn.

Rep row 1 until piece is 8½" (9", 9½") [21.8 (23, 24.3) cm] from beg. Sl st over 2 sts, ch 2, beg patt, work 16 (17, 18) shells, end 1 hdc in next st, omit last shell, turn.

Cont patt as established on 16 (17, 18) shells until armhole is 5½" (6", 6½") [14 (15, 16.3) cm], turn.

Next row: Ch 2, * work [1 sc, ch 6, 1 sc] in next ch-2 sp (buttonhole made), [1 sc, ch 2, 1 sc] in next ch-2 sp, rep from * one time more, end [1 sc, ch 6, 1 sc] in next ch-2 sp, 1 hdc in tch; fasten off.

FRONT

Work same as back until armhole is 4" (10 cm).

Shape neck as foll: work patt as established on first 6 shells, ch 2, turn.

Next row: Dec 1 st at neck edge by working 1 sc in first sp, do not complete little shell, work rem 5 shells, turn.

Work patt as established on first 5 shells, sk last sc, work 1 hdc in tch. You now have 5 shells. Cont to work patt as established on 5 shells until armhole is 5½" (6", 6½") [14 (15, 16.3) cm]; fasten off.

Sk center 4 (5, 6) shells, join yarn, work rem 6 shells to correspond.

SLEEVES

Make 2.

Foundation row: With 6/G hook, ch 34 (36, 38). Work patt same as back on 15 (16, 17) shells for 2" (5 cm).

Next row: Change to 8/H hook, and cont patt for 3" (7.5 cm) more.

First inc row: Inc 1 st each side as foll: ch 2 (counts as hdc), work 1 hdc in same st, work patt to end, work 2 hdc in last hdc.

Work in patt, keeping 2 hdc each side, for 2" (5 cm) more.

Second inc row: Ch 2 (counts as hdc), work 1 hdc in same st, 1 hdc in next st, cont shell patt across, 2 hdc in next to last hdc, 1 hdc in tch, turn. You now have 3 hdc on each side of shell patt.

Mini-shell pattern is made up of single crochet, two chains, single crochet. In each row, the shells are worked into the chain spaces of the row below. One row of the shell pattern is worked around the sweater bottom and ends of the sleeves to create a picot edge.

Next row: Ch 2 (counts as hdc), work new shell bet next 2 hdc, cont shell patt across, work new shell bet last 2 hdc, 1 hdc in tch, turn.

Cont in new patt of 17 (18, 19) shells until sleeve is 10½" (11", 11½") [26.7 (28, 29.3) cm]; fasten off.

FINISHING
1. Weave in ends, using tapestry needle.
2. Tack front to back at outer shoulder edges.
3. Fold each sleeve in half, center and pin at shoulder seam, sew in place.
4. Sew underarm seams.
5. Work neck trim: with 6/G hook, join yarn at left front neck edge, * ch 3, work 1 sc in next st, rep from * around front neck edge only; fasten off.
6. Work bottom and cuff border: join yarn at seam, RS facing you, ch 2, * work 1 sc in center ch of next shell, ch 2, 1 sc in next st, rep from * around, end Sl st to top of beg ch 2; fasten off.
7. Sew on buttons to correspond to lps.

Cable Loop Hat

Kids look so cute in bright, cheerful hats. The fun-to-hook cable loops on this rectangular hat add interesting texture. They are simply a series of chain loops that are intertwined and caught in place on the last row to form the cable.

HAT

After the first 6 rows, you will change color every 4 rows. Do not break off yarn each time, but carry loosely up sides.

Foundation row: With MC, ch 57. Starting in second ch from hook, work 1 sc in each ch across, turn—56 sts.

Row 1 (RS): Ch 1 (counts as sc), sk first st, work 1 sc in each of next 54 sts, 1 sc in top of tch, turn.

Row 2: Rep row 1.

Row 3: Ch 1, sk first st, work 1 sc in next st, * ch 12, 1 sc in each of next 4 sts, rep from * 13 times more, end 1 sc in next st, 1 sc in top of tch, turn—14 ch-12 lps.

Rows 4, 5, and 6: Keeping lps to front of work, ch 1, sk first st, work 1 sc in each st across, 1 sc in top of tch, turn.

Rows 7, 8, 9, and 10: Pull up lp with CC, rep rows 3, 4, 5, and 6 with CC.

Rep last 8 rows 2 times more. Before completing last row, ch lps tog by pulling each lp through the one below, beg at bottom row. Crochet through top lp of each cable row as you come to it, when completing last row of sc.

CABLE LOOP HAT

YARN

Medium-weight acrylic/wool yarn

Shown: Encore by Plymouth, 75% acrylic/25% wool, 3.5 oz (100 g)/200 yd (184 m): Medium Blue #4045 (MC), 1 skein; Green #3335 (CC), 1 skein

HOOK

9/I (5.5 mm)

STITCH USED

Single crochet

GAUGE

14 sc = 4" (10 cm)

NOTIONS

Tapestry needle

3" (7.5 cm) piece of cardboard

FINISHED SIZE

16½" (41.8 cm) head circumference

Chain loops, worked every five rows in alternating colors, hang free as you crochet the hat. Each column of loops is chained together from the bottom up and caught in the top row of stitches.

TASSELS

Cut 4 pieces of yarn for ties, each 12" (30.5 cm) long; set aside. Wind yarn around 3" (7.5 cm) piece of cardboard 25 times. Tie one end securely, leaving tails for tying tassel to hat. Cut other end. Wrap another tie around tassel ½" (1.3 cm) from tied end to form knob. Let ends of this tie fall into tassel; trim ends even. Repeat for second tassel.

FINISHING

1. Weave in ends, using tapestry needle.
2. Bring narrow ends together and sew seam.
3. Center seam at the back of the hat; sew top seam.
4. Tie tassels to top corners.

Multicolor Hoodie

MULTICOLOR HOODIE

Colorful, wonderfully soft yarn, simple stitches, and minimum finishing make this cardigan so special. It's roomy to make for easy layering, and the turned-up cuffs give some growing room.

YARN
Lightweight rayon yarn

Shown: Beaded Rayon by Blue Heron, 100% rayon, 8 oz (227 g)/500 yd (460 m): Daffodil, 2 skeins

HOOKS
5/F (3.75 mm)
6/G (4 mm)

STITCHES USED
Single crochet
Double crochet

GAUGE
15 dc or 15 sc = 4" (10 cm) using 6/G hook

NOTIONS
Tapestry needle
Six buttons, ¾" (2 cm) diameter
Hand-sewing needle
Thread

FINISHED SIZE
18 months (24 months, 2T)
Chest size: 26" (28", 30") [66 (71, 76) cm]

Multicolor rayon yarn in alternating rows of single and double crochet form the body, sleeves, and hood. Multiple rows of single crochet form the front bands. Chain hood tie is laced through the row ends around the hood.

BODY

Fronts and back are made all in one piece.

Foundation: Using 6/G hook, ch 94 (100, 106). Starting in second ch from hook, work 1 sc in each ch across, turn—93 (99, 105) sc.

Row 1: Ch 3 (counts as dc), sk first sc, work 1 dc in each of next 91 (97, 103) sc, 1 dc in top of tch, turn—93 (99, 105) dc.

Row 2: Ch 1, sk first dc, work 1 sc in each of next 91 (97, 103) dc, 1 sc in top of tch, turn—93 (99, 105) sc.

Rep rows 1 and 2 until piece is 9$\frac{1}{2}$" (10", 10$\frac{1}{2}$") [24.3 (25.5, 26.7) cm] from beg, ending with dc row, turn.

Divide for fronts and back as foll:
Left front: ch 1, sk first st, work sc across 20 (22, 23) sts, turn. Ch 3, sk first sc, work 1 dc on each of next 18 (20, 21) sc, 1 dc in tch, turn.

Keep patt as established on these 21 (23, 24) sts until front is 4$\frac{1}{2}$" (5", 5$\frac{1}{2}$") [11.5 (12.7, 14) cm], ending at arm side, turn.

Work patt on 13 (14, 15) sts for 2 rows only; fasten off left front.

Right front: join yarn 21 (23, 24) sts in from front edge, and work to correspond to left front.

Back: sk 4 sts from left front, join yarn, and work sc to within 4 sts of right front—43 (45, 49) sts.

Work patt until same length as front to shoulders. Sew shoulder seams.

HOOD

Starting at top of right front, RS facing you, with 6/G hook, work in sc. Pick up 15 sts along neck to shoulder seam, inc in every other st; pick up 30 sts along back of neck; pick up 15 along other front—60 sts in all for all sizes.

Work in patt (1 row sc, 1 row dc) until hood sides are 9" (9½", 9½") [23 (24.3, 24.3) cm] from beg, ending with dc row.

Next row: Sl st across 24 sts, ch 1, work 1 sc in each of next 12 sts, turn.

Working on these 12 sts only to center panel of hood, cont patt until panel is 6" (15 cm); fasten off. Align center panel to sides and sew seams to form hood.

SLEEVES

Foundation row: With 5/F hook, ch 33 (35, 37). Work in same patt as body for 6 rows.

Next row: Change to 6/G hook. Inc 1 st each side as foll: ch 1, sk first st, work 2 sc in next st, work sc across to last 2 sts, work 2 sc in next st, 1 sc in top of tch, turn.

Cont to work in patt, inc 1 st each side every eighth row 5 times more—44 (46, 48) sts.

Work even until sleeve is 11½" (12", 12½") [29.3 (30.5, 31.8) cm]; fasten off.

FINISHING

1. Fold sleeves in half, center and pin at shoulder seam, sew in place.
2. Sew underarm seams. Weave in ends, using tapestry needle.
3. Work front bands and hood trim (see below).
4. Using double strand of yarn, ch 150, fasten off. Weave the chain in and out of stitches at the edge of the hood.
5. Sew on buttons to correspond to buttonholes.

FRONT BANDS AND HOOD TRIM

Starting at top of left front, RS facing you, with 5/F hook, pick up 54 (56, 58) sts along front edge, ch 1, turn. Work 5 more rows sc on these sts; fasten off.

Join yarn at bottom of right front, pick up 54 (56, 58) sts to top of right front, ch 1, turn. Work 2 more rows of sc on these sts.

Make buttonholes on fourth row as foll: work 1 (2, 3) sc, * ch 2, sk 2, 1 sc in each of next 8 sts, rep from * across, end last rep with 1, (2, 3) sc. On fifth row, work in sc, making 2 sc in each ch-2 sp. Work 2 more rows sc; do not fasten off.

Cont around hood, picking up 30 (32, 34) sts to center panel, pick up 14 in center panel, pick up 30 (32, 34) sts down other side, cont in sc down left front; fasten off.

Crochet Stitches

SLIP KNOT AND CHAIN

All crochet begins with a chain, into which is worked the foundation row for your piece. To make a chain, start with a slip knot. To make a slip knot, make a loop several inches from the end of the yarn, insert the hook through the loop, and catch the tail with the end **(1)**. Draw the yarn through the loop on the hook **(2)**. After the slip knot, start your chain. Wrap the yarn over the hook (yarn over), and catch it with the hook. Draw the yarn through the loop on the hook. You have now made 1 chain. Repeat the process to make a row of chains. When counting chains, do not count the slip knot at the beginning or the loop that is on the hook **(3)**.

SLIP STITCH

The slip stitch is a very short stitch, which is mainly used to join 2 pieces of crochet together when working in rounds. To make a slip stitch, insert the hook into the specified stitch, wrap the yarn over the hook **(1)**, and then draw the yarn through the stitch and the loop already on the hook **(2)**.

SINGLE CROCHET

Insert the hook into the specified stitch, wrap the yarn over the hook, and draw the yarn through the stitch so there are 2 loops on the hook **(1)**. Wrap the yarn over the hook again and draw the yarn through both loops **(2)**. When working in single crochet, always insert the hook through both top loops of the next stitch, unless the directions specify front loop or back loop only.

SINGLE CROCHET TWO STITCHES TOGETHER

This decreases the number of stitches in a row or round by 1. Insert the hook into the specified stitch, wrap the yarn over the hook, and draw the yarn through the stitch so there are 2 loops on the hook. Insert the hook through the next stitch, wrap the yarn over the hook, and draw the yarn through the stitch so there are 3 loops on the hook **(1)**. Wrap the yarn over the hook again, and draw the yarn through all the loops at once **(2).**

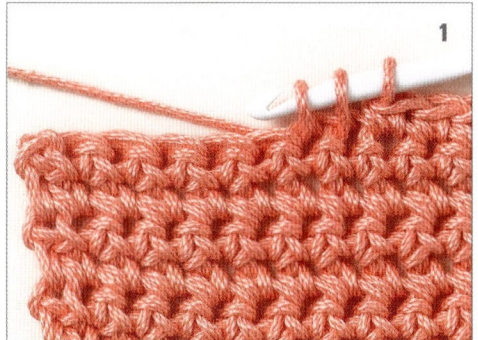 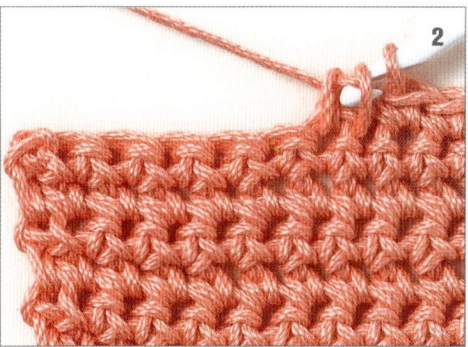

SINGLE CROCHET THROUGH THE BACK LOOP

This creates a distinct ridge on the side facing you. Insert the hook through the back loop only of each stitch, rather than under both loops of the stitch. Complete the single crochet as usual.

REVERSE SINGLE CROCHET

This stitch is usually used to create a border. At the end of a row, chain 1, but do not turn. Working backward, insert the hook into the previous stitch **(1),** wrap the yarn over the hook, and draw the yarn through the stitch so there are 2 loops on the hook. Wrap the yarn over the hook again, and draw the yarn through both loops. Continue working in the reverse direction **(2).**

HALF DOUBLE CROCHET

Wrap the yarn over the hook, insert the hook into the specified stitch, and wrap the yarn over the hook again. Draw the yarn through the stitch so there are 3 loops on the hook **(1)**. Wrap the yarn over the hook, and draw it through all 3 loops at once **(2).**

DOUBLE CROCHET

Wrap the yarn over the hook, insert the hook into the specified stitch, and wrap the yarn over the hook again. Draw the yarn through the stitch so there are 3 loops on the hook **(1)**. Wrap the yarn over the hook again, and draw it through 2 of the loops so there are now 2 loops on the hook **(2)**. Wrap the yarn over the hook again, and draw it through the last 2 loops **(3)**.

DOUBLE CROCHET TWO STITCHES TOGETHER

This decreases the number of stitches in a row or round by 1. Wrap the yarn over the hook, insert the hook into the specified stitch, and wrap the yarn over the hook again. Draw the yarn through the stitch so there are 3 loops on the hook. Wrap the yarn over the hook again, and draw it through 2 of the loops so there are now 2 loops on the hook. Wrap the yarn over the hook and pick up a loop in the next stitch, so there are now 4 loops on the hook. Wrap the yarn over the hook, draw through 2 loops, yarn over, and draw through 3 loops to complete the stitch.

DOUBLE CROCHET THROUGH THE BACK LOOP

This creates a distinct ridge on the side facing you. Wrap the yarn over the hook, and insert the hook through the back loop only of each stitch, rather than under both loops of the stitch. Complete the double crochet as usual.

TRIPLE CROCHET

Wrap the yarn over the hook twice, insert the hook into the specified stitch, and wrap the yarn over the hook again. Draw the yarn through the stitch so there are 4 loops on the hook. Wrap the yarn over the hook again **(1),** and draw it through 2 of the loops so there are now 3 loops on the hook **(2).** Wrap the yarn over the hook again, and draw it through 2 of the loops so there are now 2 loops on the hook **(3).** Wrap the yarn over the hook again, and draw it through the last 2 loops **(4).**

FRONT POST DOUBLE CROCHET

This stitch follows a row of double crochet.

Chain 3 to turn. Wrap the yarn over the hook. Working from the front, insert the hook from right to left (left to right for left-handed crocheters) under the post of the first double crochet from the previous row, and pick up a loop (shown). Wrap the yarn over the hook, and complete the stitch as a double crochet.

Left-handed.

Right-handed.

SHELL STITCH

Make 2 double crochets, chain 1, and then work 2 more double crochets in the same stitch (shown). This is often called a cluster. In the following row, work the same cluster into the space created by the chain stitch.

CHAIN LOOP FLOWERS

Rows of chain loop flowers are found in the dress bodice on page 8, the matching hat on page 14, and the cardigan sweater on page 66. The effect is best when using two different colors of yarn. In the right side set-up row, with contrasting color, three loops that will become the leaves and stem of each flower are formed by (single crochet, chain 8) 3 times in the same stitch for each flower. Working in the main color yarn and keeping the loops toward the front of the work, on the next right side row, each leaf loop is caught into the row by working a single crochet stitch through the loop into the designated stitch. The stem loop is still free at this point. In the next right side row, the stem loop is caught in place as 6 double crochet stitches are worked through the loop and into the designated stitch, also forming the blossom at the top of the stem.

CABLE STITCHES

In cable patterns, as for the sweater on page 72, pairs of raised ridges crisscross at regular intervals. The raised ridges are created with front post double crochet stitches formed around the stitches two rows below. The instructions and photographs that follow show you how to crisscross the ridges.

Follow the directions up to the front post double crochet ridge. * Skip over the next front post double crochet bar and the next single crochet, work a front post double crochet around the second front post double crochet **(1)**, single crochet in the single crochet between the two bars **(2)**, front post double crochet over the front post double crochet that was skipped **(3)**, single crochet up to the next set of ridges, and repeat from *.

PICKING UP STITCHES FOR BORDERS

Picking up stitches along the sides of a project, the row ends, is the hardest part of giving your crochet pieces a lovely finished look. It is worth the effort to practice a little to get this step just right.

The general rule of thumb is to pick up 1 stitch in every other row for single crochet **(1)**. For instance, if you have worked 20 rows of single crochet, you will pick up 10 stitches along the row ends. Pick up 1 stitch for every row for double crochet **(2)**. For instance, if you have worked 20 rows of double crochet, you will pick up 20 stitches. These guidelines work for most people, but not all. If your edges are rippling, you are picking up too many stitches; if they are pulling in, you are picking up too few stitches.

SETTING IN DROP SHOULDER SLEEVES

After the shoulder seams have been sewn, place the front and back, wrong side up, on the work surface. Fold the sleeve in half to find the center. Place the sleeve, wrong side up, alongside the armhole, and pin the center to the shoulder seam. Pin the remainder of the sleeve top in place, having each side reach the indent at the underarm. The body indents align to the row ends at the top of the sleeve. Holding the edges together, insert the yarn needle into the first stitch on the sleeve, then into the corresponding stitch on the body of garment. Continue in this manner going from side to side until the sleeve is sewn in place. Repeat for the opposite sleeve. Then sew the underarm seams from the sleeve cuffs to the bottom of the body. Turn the garment right side out.

When setting a sleeve into a garment that doesn't have side seams, fold the garment in half, wrong side out. Follow the same procedure, beginning and ending at the center of the garment underarm. Then sew the sleeve underarm seam. Turn the garment right side out.

Abbreviations

approx	approximately	**p**	picot
beg	begin/beginning	**patt**	pattern
bet	between	**pc**	popcorn
BL	back loop(s)	**pm**	place marker
BP	back post	**prev**	previous
BPdc	back post double crochet	**rem**	remain/remaining
CC	contrasting color	**rep**	repeat(s)
ch	chain	**rev sc**	reverse single crochet
ch-	refers to chain or space previously made, e.g., ch-1 space	**rnd(s)**	round(s)
		RS	right side(s)
ch lp	chain loop	**sc**	single crochet
ch-sp	chain space	**sc2tog**	single crochet 2 stitches together
CL	cluster(s)	**sk**	skip
cm	centimeter(s)	**Sl st**	slip stitch
cont	continue	**sp(s)**	space(s)
dc	double crochet	**st(s)**	stitch(es)
dc2tog	double crochet 2 stitches together	**tch**	turning chain
		tbl	through back loop(s)
dec	decrease/decreases/decreasing	**tfl**	through front loop(s)
		tog	together
FL	front loop(s)	**tr**	triple crochet
foll	follow/follows/following	**tr2tog**	triple crochet 2 together
FP	front post	**WS**	wrong side(s)
FPdc	front post double crochet	**yd**	yard(s)
FPtr	front post triple crochet	**yo**	yarn over
g	gram(s)	**yoh**	yarn over hook
hdc	half double crochet		
inc	increase/increases/increasing	**[ ]**	Work instructions within brackets as many times as directed
lp(s)	loop(s)	*****	Repeat instructions following the single asterisk as directed
m	meter(s)		
MC	main color	******	Repeat instructions between asterisks as many times as directed or repeat from a given set of instructions
mm	millimeter(s)		
oz	ounce(s)		